The Economic System of China
中国的经济制度

中国的经济制度
The Economic System of China

张五常经典作品系列
神州大地增订版 英文原著·作者亲译

张五常 著

中信出版集团·北京

图书在版编目（CIP）数据

中国的经济制度 / 张五常著. -- 2 版. -- 北京：
中信出版社，2017.12（2022.7 重印）
ISBN 978-7-5086-6750-8

Ⅰ. ①中… Ⅱ. ①张… Ⅲ. ①中国经济－经济制度－
研究 Ⅳ. ① F121

中国版本图书馆 CIP 数据核字 (2016) 第 231997 号

中国的经济制度

著　　者：张五常
出版发行：中信出版集团股份有限公司
　　　　　（北京市朝阳区惠新东街甲 4 号富盛大厦 2 座　邮编　100029）
承 印 者：北京盛通印刷股份有限公司

开　　本：880mm×1230mm　1/32　　印　张：6.5　　字　数：79 千字
版　　次：2017 年 12 月第 2 版　　　　印　次：2022 年 7 月第 12 次印刷
书　　号：ISBN 978-7-5086-6750-8
定　　价：36.00 元

版权所有·侵权必究
如有印刷、装订问题，本公司负责调换。
服务热线：400-600-8099
投稿邮箱：author@citicpub.com

This paper is dedicated to Ronald Coase, whose idea on the clear delineation of rights inspired the economic awakening of a great nation, and to celebrate the 30th anniversary of what must be the greatest program for economic reform in history.

谨以此文献给罗纳德·科斯。
他那权利要有清楚界定的理念，
唤醒了一个庞大的国家。
并以此祝贺历史上最伟大的
经济改革三十周年。

The author is grateful to Ronald Coase, Lars Werin, Yoram Barzel and Michael Cheung for their detailed comments on various drafts of this paper.

感谢科斯、沃因、巴泽尔和张滔。他们细读了此文的初稿,提供了意见。

Table of Contents 目录

神州增订版序 11
学术生涯的终结 15
时代文章 23

The Economic System of China

I.   The 'China Question' 31
II.   The Impact of Ideas 38
III.   A General Concept of Contracts 44
IV.   Evolution of the Responsibility Contract 53
V.   The Manifestation of the Responsibility Contracts and the Rise of the Competing Xians 59
VI.   The Sharecropping Nature of the Xian System 65
VII. The Sharing Formula and Its Effects 74
VIII. Economic Interpretation of the Xian Phenomenon 79
IX.   Side Effects of Xian Competition 87
X.   The Monetary System of China and the Rise of the RMB 92

XI. Concluding Remarks 100
An Unhappy Epilogue..104

中国的经济制度

第一节：中国的问题..115
第二节：思想的冲击..121
第三节：合约的一般概念..127
第四节：承包责任合约的演进..136
第五节：承包合约的扩张与县际竞争的兴起..............................141
第六节：县制度的佃农分成..146
第七节：分成方程式的效果..154
第八节：县现象的经济解释..158
第九节：县际竞争的其他效应..166
第十节：中国的货币制度与人民币的兴起................................170
第十一节：结语..178
不愉快的后记..182

芝大研讨会科斯的前言后语
Conference Opening and Closing Remarks
by Ronald Coase..189

神州增订版序

　　回顾平生,在学术研究上我老老实实地走了一段漫长而又艰苦的路。一九六七写好博士论文《佃农理论》,二〇〇八写好《中国的经济制度》,相距四十一年,二者皆可传世,思想史上没有谁的智力可以在自己的顶峰维持那么久。上苍对我格外仁慈,给我有得天独厚之感。

　　也回顾平生,自己认为足以传世的英语文章约九篇之谱。一般朋友举《佃农》为首,科斯选《蜜蜂的神话》,阿尔钦选《座位票价》,而巴泽尔则肯定《价格管制理论》是无与伦比的。我自己呢?选《中国的经济制度》!两年前写好初稿时我那样想,两年后的今天我还是那样想。似浅实深,这里独立成书的《制度》一文牵涉到的话题广泛,细节多,史实长达三十年,合约理论的分析达到了一个前不见古人的层面,而其中好几处要靠机缘巧合,或时来运到,才找到答案。没有任何"缺环",完整若天衣无缝也。读者要记住,《制度》一文其实写到二〇〇七,分析的是新《劳动合同法》

引进之前的经济奇迹。

学术过于专注有机会发神经，而我的集中力惊人，往往一发难收。我因而喜欢这里那里分心一下，于是搞摄影、练书法、写散文、好收藏，尝试过的投资或生意无数。这些行为惹来非议，而我喜欢到街头巷尾跑的习惯，使一些无聊之辈认为我早就放弃了学术，不是昔日的史提芬·张云云。这些人不知道经济学的实验室是真实的世界，不多到那里观察算不上是科学。至于那些认为我转向研究中国是浪费了天赋的众君子，属坐井观天，既不知天高，也不知地厚。是的，我这一辈在西方拜师学艺的人知道，在国际学术上中国毫不重要，没有半席之位可言。也怪不得，在学问上炎黄子孙没有一家之言，恐怕不止二百年了。今天老人家西望，竟然发觉那里的经济大师不怎么样。不懂中国，对经济的认识出现了一个大缺环，算不上真的懂经济。

《中国的经济制度》这本英、中二语的书，在香港出版过三次。这次攻进内地，应该有点前途。为此我补做了两件事。其一是在正文之前我加进两篇有关的文章，介绍正文的重要性。其二是在正文中我作了些补充。此文早就修改过无数次。科斯要把该文与其他文章一起结集在美国出版，问我还有没有需要修改的地方。我反复重读，找不到有什么地方要改，但有几处不妨多说几句，尤其是在第八节之后加了四段我认为是重要的。就让国内的同学先读这些补充吧。

是为序。

张五常
二〇〇九年八月一日

学术生涯的终结

张五常　　二〇〇八年九月二十六日

　　为科斯的芝大会议提供的《中国的经济制度》一文，是我在学术上的严谨论著中最后的作品了。不会再写。专栏文字还会继续一些日子吧。不少旧文需要整理，三卷本的《经济解释》还要修改，但正规的学术文章——结构慎重、注脚详尽的那种——我是不会再染指的了。七十二岁，还有其他有趣的要做——书法也愈来愈有看头——以《中国的经济制度》终结学术生涯既有意思，也很痛快。

　　多年来我担心思考能力走下坡自己不知道，写出令人尴尬的学术分析。一些老了的朋友遇到这样的不幸。就算自己得天独厚，跟大自然斗法是斗不过的。《中国》一文是得意之作，向前看，这样水平的学术文章自己无法重复，再向前走，下坡必然，就此终结，仰天大笑，不亦潇洒乎？

　　我的《佃农理论》发表于一九六八，《中国的经济制度》二〇〇八，刚好四十年。加上《佃农》之前的创意争取，是四十三年。施蒂格勒曾经以出版日期算，从一个经济学者的第一件重要作品到最后重要的，依稀记得，最长不到三十年。我达四十，上苍网开一面，于愿足矣。

二十个月前，科斯要搞一个中国经济改革的研讨会议，问我意见。我想，他九十六岁了，还能搞什么呢？当时大家都没有想到他选的日子刚好是中国经改的三十周年。我回信说："如果你要搞，我可以提供一篇题为《中国的经济制度》的文章。"以为他只是说说，会议多半开不成，文章不一定真的要写。但我可不是信口开河。当时我肯定地知道《中国的经济制度》会是一篇大文，之前没有尝试过那么重要的。二〇〇四年底我大致上解通了中国经济制度的密码，知道这制度史无先例，写得深入全面此文的重要性自成一家，但题材复杂，牵涉到的理论与事实非常广泛，还有很多细节要再作调查或复核，恐怕自己不会有需要的魄力了。说说无妨，建议无妨，但真的动笔是另一回事。

殊不知个多月后，科斯的助手传来一个暂定的会议程序表。我的《中国的经济制度》开场，给我两个小时，跟着是两个诺奖得主评论该文，加上其他人的讨论占了整个上午，其他提供文章的是空白格子，要填上，每人仅得二十分钟。科斯跟着来信，说要以我的开场文章引导整个研讨会议的发展。一九九一在瑞典见过他，当时我的女儿刚进大学，今天已有两个懂得欺负我的孩子了。难道科斯忘记了我早就是个老人家？昔日他欣赏我的来去纵横的思想，还在吗？他怎可以假设我还宝刀未老？

我逼着去信，说："答应你的文章我会写，但不少被邀请的人会来自中国，费用不少，会议的经费怎样，要我帮助吗？"他回信说不需要资助，他自己的基金足够。我想，那应该主要是他的诺贝尔奖金，很感动。跟着想，我欠他，中国也欠他，大家来日无多，他要搞，我就舍命陪君子吧。于是给他信，说："我答应你的文章将会是我平生最重要的作品！"

是经过很长的调查与思考的时日了。一九七九我开始跟进中国的发展，时疏时密，没有中断过。八五年起深圳与北京的朋友给予很多方便，需要的资料有求必应。到了八十年代后期，发展愈来愈复杂，也很混乱，要到好些年后回顾，大手而又武断地简化，才得到一个自己认为是可靠的大略，怎样取舍我要集中于制度的发展，不少话题要被拨开了。我是一九九七才惊觉到中国经济制度的重点是地区之间的激烈竞争，史无先例。当然，地区竞争某程度世界各地都有，但中国的是一种特别的生意竞争，外地没有出现过。

我要到二〇〇三年才肯定县是地区竞争的主角，这种竞争是公司与公司之间的竞争，为何如此不容易解释。复杂难明的问题多得很，而最后一个难关要到二〇〇四年底，深夜仿佛睡着时突然想到一九六六年读到的马歇尔的一个注脚，才解通整体。要是我没有从始就跟进中国的经改发展，没有亲自替家传的抛光蜡到内地找地方设厂，没有深入地研究过佃农分成、公司性质、合约理论等，我不可能解通中国经济制度的密码。

解通是一回事，写出来是更头痛的另一回事了。不打算写出来，因为认为要用一本书的篇幅才能处理，而自己老了，体力应付不了。另一方面，我熟知科斯的固执品性：只要还健在，他说要做的一定会做，答应了他我是走投无路的。以一篇文章处理，反复考虑多处删减，一篇长文的结构想出来了。

重要的困难是要有一个一般性的理论来支撑着整篇文章。为此，去年四月起我一连写了十一篇关于经济学的缺环，是基于跟进中国的发展多年的思维，补充了自己早期的制度研究。这十一篇发表后，再多想两个星期，把心一横，我决定放弃自己多年来用惯了的产权分析，转用以合约约束竞争的角度，而交易费用则变为约束竞争的费用了。

有这样的需要，因为中国的经济制度是一连串的承包合约的组合——整个国家的经济制度是一个庞大的合约组织。这个有一般性的理论是后来文章中的第三节，是原创，科斯喜爱，认为重要，建议我把该节起名为《合约的一般概念》。这是制度经济学的一个没有人到过的层面了。

去年七月开始动笔。知道要一气呵成，但年逾七十，短暂的记忆大不如前，是长文，思维的连贯性不可以写一阵停一阵。于是决定不睡觉地一口气写了三个星期，减了五磅，写好了自己满意的初稿。其间每天稍事休息多次，昼夜不分，足不出户。

《中国的经济制度》的写法跟我以前的学术论著还有另一点不同。那就是我只写给科斯一个人读。四十年前在芝大校园我跟他怎样对话，这次动笔就怎样说。我要向他"汇报"一下从中国的研究得到的收获。此前对他说过，我认为新制度经济学的发展走进了一个死胡同，再不是有趣的学问了。一士谔谔，思想杀出了重围，何处觅知音哉？科斯还在，大家有共通的语言，高山流水一番有意思吧。

去年八月初稿传了给科斯，过了一天叫他不要读，因为将会有第二稿。他读第二稿后显得兴奋，对助手形容为 powerful（后来蒙代尔在芝大评论该文时用上同一个字）。科斯跟着给我的信，只说："不用担心，你的文章完全满足了我的要求。"

　　个多月后，科斯给我一封长信，说他和助手一起花了几天再细读我的文稿，提出了二十七处认为要修改的建议，但说改不改由我。其中大部分是文字上的小修，举手之劳。有七处比较麻烦，其中三处我认为不应该改。余下来的四处怎样处理，我决定搁置几个月再想。

　　到了今年初，科斯催促要看第三稿。我见时间还多，再等。四月修改，第三稿花了两个星期，琐碎耗时的是加进五十三个注脚。四月底科斯收到第三稿，更满意了，对助手说我改了很多。其实不多，我只是把四处他不满意的地方再写，也删去了部分不易懂但不是那么重要的。没有听过科斯给其他文章更高的评价，但他认为该文难读，对读者的要求甚高，同时又说这难度看来是需要的。

　　科斯没有读过第四稿。那是在正式"交卷"前我从头复核一次所有用上的资料，作了几处小修。还会有第五稿的，那是要将一处常被误解的再加澄清，而一个重点我认为不言自明，但读者一般看不出其重要性：资源使用的权利界定（私产）重要，但不同的合约组织可以有很大的效率差别，单靠市场的自由选择是不可以达到中国制度的合约组织的。自由市场不成，计划经济也不成。成事要靠经济压力——资源贫乏十三亿人要吃饭的压力——也要有一个懂得疏导交通的政权。

中国的经济制度是个奇迹，既精彩又重要。一脚踏中这个题材是万中无一的机缘巧合，而我平生所学刚好全部用上。天助我也！

时代文章

张五常　二〇〇八年十月七日

为科斯写的《中国的经济制度》是我平生无数的中英二语的作品中,唯一的还没有动笔就知道是大文,肯定是。作为一件经济学作品,其题材的重要性难得一遇。我想得通透,分析反复多次,资料大部分是自己多年的观察。困难是题材复杂,牵涉到的范围广泛。答应了科斯不能不写,苦思良久终于想出可以处理整个话题的一篇长文的结构。

从他评论的细节看,九十七岁的科斯读得清楚明白。数十年来他和我在经济学上的思维一致有助。其他从事新制度经济学的朋友如巴泽尔、德姆塞茨、诺斯等人,今天和我的沟通就有点沙石了。阔别了四分之一个世纪,大家分道扬镳,思想的角度不同,层面有别,不是三言两语就可以把思维汇合在一起的。都老了,谁对谁错,孰优孰劣,再不是值得争论的话题。我深信,有朝一日,后学的对经济解释再有兴趣的话,《中国的经济制度》一文会教他们很多。科斯细读该文后对一位朋友说，当年催促张五常回到香港研究中国是他平生做得最对的一件事。另一方面，一些没有读过经济的朋友可以不管文内的理论或概念而明大概，尤其是那些有经验的干部及多年在内地投资设厂的。没有成见重要。

动笔前就肯定是一篇大文，因为意识到该文是一个大时代转变的产品。即是说，没有经历着这大时代的转变，该文不可能写出来。回顾平生比较严谨的学术论著，有七八件行内朋友认为是经典的，没有一件反映着自己生存的时代。师友中没有谁有这样的运气。

西方经济学发展了二百多年，没有大时代转变写不出来的大作只三件。其一是市场与国际贸易的兴起惹来管制，亚当·斯密一七七六发表《国富论》。其二是大资本家的出现惹来贫富分化，马克思一八六七发表《资本论》。其三是金融业的兴起惹来大萧条，凯恩斯一九三六发表《通论》。

我们今天面对的大时代转变，比上述三君子面对的来得远为庞大、复杂。恨不得自己还年轻，有魄力仿效亚当·斯密写一本巨著。与此无缘，写出来的《中国的经济制度》只是其中一章，风水有灵，这章是重要的。

我们要怎样看面对的大时代转变呢？重点在

哪里？是地球一体化吗？是地球暖化吗？是科技的突飞猛进吗？是互联网与资讯传达的奇迹吗？又或者是目前吵得怕人的金融大风暴？这一切皆非等闲——我们身处的大时代无疑是多事之秋。但我认为这些都不是重点。个人之见，我们面对的大时代转变，重点是地球上有二十亿以上的贫困人口，为了改进生活一起站起来参与国际产出竞争。惊天地，泣鬼神，人类历史没有出现过。

这样看，中国重要，因为整个大转变是三十年前由中国发起的。一九九一苏联解体，人类就进入了一个大时代。除了近几年人民币的处理失当与去年新《劳动合同法》的引进，中国着着占了先机，其示范起了作用，把地球上的无数穷人带动了。

中国的发展有两大奇迹，不容易相信，但真的出现了。其一是在极端困难的九十年代——从高通胀急转为通缩的年代——长江三角洲大约八年就超越了起步早十年的珠江三角洲。其二是二〇〇〇通缩终结后的七年，中国农民的收入增长率，每年高达百分之二十，工作年龄的农民十个有七个转到工商业去了。大举农转工的困难专家学者说过无数次。明治维新时日本出现过，六十年代台湾地区出现过，七十年代韩国也出现过。都有看头，但比起中国大陆，从速度与气势衡量，皆小巫见大巫，不可以相提并论。

是中国的发展带动了整个地球的穷人站起来，争先恐后地转到工业去。一九九六年我就看得准，发表了《缺粮说》。但中国的奇迹究竟是由什么促成的呢？说私产重要，那当然，这是八十年代我极力主张而北京的朋友容易理解的把资产使用的权利界定清楚的发展。然而，说得上是有私产但发展平平无奇的国家不少。中国经济的奇迹发展不是八十年代，而是九十年代。后者有大贪污及大肃贪，有大通胀及大调控，有大通缩及楼价下降了四分之三。乱七八糟。偏偏是在这样的情况下，中国的经济就像一只凤凰从火灰中飞跃起来了。为什么呢？这应该是我们面对的大时代转变中的最重要一课，奇怪行内的朋友没有一个注意到。《中国的经济制度》提供了一个完整的解释。

亚当·斯密的《国富论》受到大时代的影响，解释了市场与贸易带来的利益，从而影响了大时代。马克思的《资本论》受到大时代的影响，但"剩余价值"解释不了贫富分化，也影响了大时代。凯恩斯的《通论》受到大时代的影响，但解释不了大萧条，再也影响了大时代。这些影响是好是坏，是另一回事。

我的《中国的经济制度》也是受到大时代的影

响，成功地解释了中国，可惜只算是一章，对大时代的影响不会有谁察觉到吧。传世数十年应该没有问题。只发表了三个月，一家搜索引擎说该文被引用或提及的次数（不是点击率）达八万五千八百次。

是多么不公平的世界。昔日王羲之说一句"群贤毕至"，李白说一句"浮生若梦"，苏东坡说一句"逝者如斯"，今天的炎黄子孙只要读书识字，没有谁背不出来。同样，莫扎特写下的音乐，不仅今天普及，恐怕只要人类存在，小孩子也唱得出来。牛顿的三大定律与爱因斯坦的相对论，懂也好，不懂也好，人类会持久地朗朗上口。

经济学者可没有这样的运情！做研究生时我佩服得五体投地的经济学文章，今天的后起之秀一般没有听过。就是科斯一九六〇发表的施蒂格勒认为是整个二十世纪最重要的经济思想，被引用的次数这些年跌得厉害。一些朋友要在今年十一月举办"佃农理论四十年"的研讨会议，只不过是要对一个还活着的老人打个招呼，是行内的习惯吧。

亚当·斯密还在，马克思还在，凯恩斯还在。这三君子不容易被忘记，因为他们的主要作品不仅由一个大时代的转变促成，他们也有能耐把自己写进历史去。

The Economic System of China

The Economic System of China

I. The 'China Question'

Personally, I am inclined to date the beginning of economic reform in China as 1980. I saw no sign of reform when re-visiting Guangzhou in the fall of 1979 after many years away. Beijing officials and future historians will no doubt choose 1978 as the beginning. Here one can be exact: December 22, 1978. On that day, the 3rd Plenary Session of the 11th Central Committee of the Communist Party of China announced a decision of immense importance. With this dating the present conference on China, arranged by Ronald Coase, takes on a special meaning: It marks the 30th anniversary of what must be the greatest program for economic reform in history.

The 3rd Plenary Session decided on two things. First, China was to open up to advance economic development; second, Deng Xiaoping was restored to power. At the time, not many people gave credence to the proclamations. On economic matters, similar ambitions had been expressed before. As to Deng's return to power, this was his third time. Though Deng was explicitly invested with *top* powers, there were comrades senior to him who opposed market economics, and seniority was something that counted in China in 1978. Who could tell what may happen? Deng may soon be down again.

In the summer of 1979, Arthur Seldon of the Institute of Economic Affairs asked me to write on China's economic prospects. He said the Thatcher administration was interested in an academic analysis. I went to Guangzhou in the fall, and have followed with increasing interest China's economic development and transformation ever since. In 1981, I came to the realization that constraints were changing sharply in the country, and wrote for Arthur a piece long enough to be a pamphlet. Published in 1982, *Will China Go Capitalist?*[1] predicted in no uncertain terms: Yes, China will go capitalist! The year's delay was caused by criticisms from friends and colleagues. Yoram Barzel, my closest colleague in Seattle, disagreed with the answer, but he felt that the theoretical section was so good that it would be a shame if the manuscript did not go into print.

In retrospect, the accuracy of my prediction surprised friends and colleagues, and I myself have been surprised by the speed of change that followed. Nearly thirty years of continuous and rapid economic growth have surpassed the Meiji Restoration era in Japan, and occurring in a country as large, as populous, and as complex as China, it is almost beyond belief. Moreover, as this miracle unfolded the Chinese had to contend with corruption, a

---

[1] Institute of Economic Affairs (London: 1982), Hobart Paper 84.

D-grade judicial system, controls on freedom of speech and beliefs, education and health care which were neither public nor private, exchange controls, inconsistent policies, and 60,000 so-called riots a year. With the exception of the riot statistics — which begs a definition, as friends in different areas told me they were unable to see anything they would call a 'riot' — all the above negative things really happened.

Around 2003, several friends who knew China well complained to me regarding the country's ills and shortcomings. I replied: "Do not tell me what is wrong. I can write a thick book on what is wrong by next week. Yet despite all the problems, China has grown at such high rates and over such a long period that there is no parallel in history. Especially, do not repeat what some people believe, that corruption is good for economic development. Zhu Rongji's efforts flatly reject that hypothesis. China must have done something supremely right to produce the economic miracle we observe. What is it? That is the real question."

I explained to my friends what had puzzled me for some years in terms of the following parable. A high jumper, in the eyes of the experts, seems not to know what to do. He stumbles around and his style is clumsy. Yet he manages to jump eight feet, a world record. The man must have done something right, more right than all jumpers before. What is it? That, in a different context, is the China question.

This paper attempts an answer. It is long and

involved, as I have a history to relate and a theory to explain. To do this, I must focus on what China has done right. It suffices here to repeat again that if need be, I could write many books detailing the wrongs.

An economic miracle China truly is, since 1980. Milton Friedman once hailed the economic miracle of Hong Kong, for though its population increased 10-folds since the war, per-capita income still increased significantly. Yet the City of Shenzhen just north of Hong Kong achieved a higher growth rate, with a population which went up 45 times during a similar time span. To take another example: After five years, I could recognize hardly anything when re-visiting the town of Shaoxing. Migrant workers are reported not to be able to find their own homes when returning after a lapse of just three years. Some cities deep in the Chinese mainland resemble San Francisco, with sparkling night lights on highrise buildings. Currently, more than half of the world's new elevators are being installed in China.

Highways are constructed in China at a rate exceeding 4,000 kilometers a year, long enough to span the entire United States. In the mid-1990's, 17% of the world's construction cranes can be found in Shanghai. Sharply falling property prices notwithstanding, welders can be seen laboring on high rise structures at midnight, like stars in the sky. More office space was built in Shanghai in five years than fast-growing Hong Kong managed in fifty. In 2002 Shanghai planners abruptly restricted building heights, because they found the city sinking under the weight of real estate. The four-lane highway between Shanghai and Nanjing, empty when newly built and criticized for being a waste of money, became so congested and earned so much in tolls that five years later work was begun to double its capacity. Because tolls are charged according to the size of trucks, overloading became so severe that some roads constructed according to world-class standards are damaged in no time. Congestion occurs at each and every seaport in the country. In 2005, the world's longest and the second longest sea crossing bridges were under construction at the same time and in the same area.

A single shoe factory in Wenzhou employs 120,000 workers. That city literally produces all of the world's lighters and Christmas lightings. Yiwu, where vendors sold goods on the streets 15 years ago, now exports more than 1,000 containers a day, with purchasing agents from Korea and Africa jamming the city and pushing office rents through the roof. Who has ever heard of several thousand shops selling nothing but socks? That is Yiwu: The wholesale malls there are so huge that I took one look and sat down, for an old man like me could not handle the distance. The town of Lecong has a road selling furniture on both sides, stretching ten kilometers long. The large industrial village in Suzhou, so beautifully landscaped and filled with manufacturers of world-class brands and industrial structures of world-class designs, cropped up in the middle of paddy fields in five years. Hangzhou receives forty million tourists a year. One retail shop in that city, selling a famous brand of handbags, grosses US$80,000 on an average day.

I could go on and on describing similar phenomena, but there is no point. What one needs to add, however, is a story about Pudong, or Shanghai east of the river. I took the Friedmans there in 1993. Nothing could be seen except a row of one-story shops, reportedly built to entertain Deng Xiaoping. Milton (of course) resented any such action, pointing out government development planning would fail most of the time. Yet eight years later I took an American architect to downtown Pudong, and stunned, he observed that the high rises concentrated there may well be the best in the world. The lesson is this: For a country as big and populous as China, growing at such speed, there is plenty of room for learning by doing.[2]

---

[2] When Shanghai announced plans to build a second international airport in Pudong in 1997, skeptics argued that the old airport was not even used to capacity. The new Pudong airport began operations in 1999 with one runway, which soon proved insufficient. A second runway was added in 2005, and a third runway, with an added terminal, was built in 2008. A second runway for the old airport is now under construction, so that Shanghai ended up building one additional runway every 2.5 years.

Similar stories can be told for toll roads and bridges, where money-losers soon turned into money-makers. A friend mourned his decision to sell a section of a highway which was soon loaded with traffic. The output of a small producer of instant noodles from Taiwan increased to 30 million packages per day in five years. There was a period of about six years, from 2000 to 2006, when the investor almost could not go wrong! Unfortunately, this bullish environment has been changing for the worse, and by late 2007 it is changing rapidly.

Today, office construction continues unabated in Pudong, but at the same time many buildings stand vacant. Yet property prices there are rising. There is only one explanation for the seeming contradiction: People are waiting. They invest and wait, on the expectation that when China drops exchange and banking controls, Shanghai-Pudong will immediately become a leading financial center.

The statistics do not add up. An official friend working on them admitted that there is no way to put the figures together coherently. In 2005 Beijing substantially revised past growth rates upwards, but the adjustments did not cover dramatic improvements in the quality of products and services. What is more, the growth rates reported by nearly all provinces were higher, sometimes much higher, than Beijing's calculation of the growth rate as a whole. In 2006 the City of Guangzhou reported a spectacular increase in per capita income, but mainly because they divided total output value by the registered population and ignored the several millions of unregistered floating workers. There is no question that the livelihood of peasants has gone straight up since about 2000, but official statistics show slower per capita growth than the cities. They must have used registered population in these calculations, because nobody knows how many farm-hands have "floated" away. I believe more than one-third of the working population has been floating around the country. Not knowing the pitfalls, outside organizations have severally reported the Gini index of China to be rising dangerously. These reports miss the target by miles.

II. The Impact of Ideas

Robert Mundell, honorary citizen of Beijing and Coase admirer, on hearing that the great man is organizing a conference on China, suggested that someone should write a paper eulogizing Coase's contributions and that I should be the person to do so. I have been invited by Coase to write this lead-off paper on China's economic reforms, not on himself. However, it would still be appropriate to begin with the impact of Coasian economics. In doing so, I cannot avoid involving myself, because I alone was responsible for introducing Coase's ideas to the Chinese people.

I published my first Chinese article in Hong Kong in October 1979, on "One Thousand Rules, Ten Thousand Rules, in Economics There is Only One Rule."[3] This strange title was adopted in response to a piece I read a year earlier, written by a noted Chinese economist, Sun Yefang, on "One Thousand Rules, Ten Thousand Rules, Economic Value is the First Rule."[4] During the cultural revolution, Sun made such a statement and was imprisoned for seven

---

[3] 张五常,《千规律, 万规律, 经济规律仅一条》, 一九七九年十月《信报财经月刊》。

[4] 孙冶方,《千规律, 万规律, 价值规律第一条》, 一九七八年十月《光明日报》。

years. I of course was sympathetic, but disagreed with Sun regarding his Marxian notions of value and price. My article elaborated just one point: Competition is inevitable under scarcity; to determine winners or losers criteria are essential; of the numerous criteria that can be applied, only market price entails no dissipation of rent.[5] The argument considered various alternatives, such as allocation through queuing, seniority, etc., and showed that all led to incremental wastage in terms of rent dissipation. But not so on the criterion of market pricing, and the use of market price is uniquely associated with private

---

[5] The important thesis of the dissipation of rent originated in the analysis of common property resource usage, where rental value may be competed away or replaced by a higher cost of use when the resource is subject to unrestrained common exploitation. I have further argued that, so long as the market price is not used or is suppressed by policy measures, some other criteria must emerge to determine the outcome of competition, and any such criterion would lead to rent dissipation. The interpretation of economic behavior in terms of rent dissipation is truly important, but it has been neglected by the profession. In particular, I have found the approach to be very useful when analyzing constraints arising from transaction costs.

On the literature, see Frank H. Knight, "Some Fallacies in the Interpretation of Social Cost," *Quarterly Journal of Economics* (August 1924); H. Scott Gordon, "The Economic Theory of a Common Property Resource: The Fishery," *Journal of Political Economy* (April 1954); Steven N. S. Cheung, "The Structure of a Contract and the Theory of a Non-exclusive Resource," *Journal of Law and Economics* (April 1970); Idem, "A Theory of Price Control," *Journal of Law and Economics* (April 1974).

property.⁶

Years later I discovered that this article had been widely read in Beijing, and according to many friends it had something to do with China's later practice of charging prices for just about everything. A systematic exposition of Coase's ideas on the clear delineation of rights and transaction costs first appeared in Chinese in 1982, in a translation of my IEA paper, *Will China Go Capitalist?*.⁷

I began Chinese writing in earnest in November 1983. "The Communist System as Viewed through the Coase Theorem," in which the example of cattle raising and wheat farming is discussed in detail, appeared in January 1984.⁸ I have now written 1,500 Chinese articles, about half on economics. Pieces on economic reform and policies come to about one-third of the total. But I am no reformer. However, having nearly starved to death as a

---

⁶ Using price is costly, but as a criterion of competition it is unique in that no further rent is dissipated. For the costs of using price, see R. H. Coase, "The Nature of the Firm," *Economica* (November 1937); George J. Stigler, "The Economics of Information," *Journal of Political Economy* (June 1961); Steven N. S. Cheung, "The Contractual Nature of the Firm," *Journal of Law and Economics* (April 1983).

⁷ 张五常，《中国会走向资本主义的道路吗？》，一九八二，重刊于张五常，《中国的前途》，一九八五年八月初版，再版多次，今天由香港花千树出版。

⁸ 张五常，《从科斯定律看共产政制》一九八四年一月二十七日发表于《信报》，转刊于《卖桔者言》，后者一九八四年十一月初版，再版无数次，今天由香港花千树出版。

boy in Guangxi, there is no hiding the fact that after surviving to become an old man I do care. It is not important whether people agree with me, so long as they read what I write. I believe anyone who reads another's writings must to some degree be influenced.

There was no better time, no better place, and perhaps no better sales person, than this writer in popularizing the ideas of Coase to the Chinese in the 1980s. The ideological gate was beginning to swing open: Comrades knew what they had believed in did not work, and were looking for something new. I was appointed to the Chair of Economics of the University of Hong Kong in May 1982, the best position at that time to follow China's development. I knew Ronald's works by heart, and people knew he was a good friend of mine.[9] I was expert on Chinese culture and history, so comrades could not tell me that I did not understand China, as they routinely told outsiders. I could write in Chinese, and soon developed a style people say was popular though distinctive. On top of all this are the seminal ideas of Coase, which at that time were easy to sell. Had China then been like the China now, I would be out of luck.

---

[9] During the 1980 American Economic Association annual meeting in Detroit, Coase urged me to return to China because he heard that the country was considering reform, and he believed I was the best person to impart knowledge on the operation of economic systems to the Chinese people. A few months later, I was informed that the Chair of Economics at the University of Hong Kong would soon be open. I was appointed to that chair in May 1982, and retired eighteen years later.

First is the idea of transaction costs. Chinese living under the earlier regime were all too familiar with such chores and headaches as memorizing political slogans, waiting in line, making connections, dealing through the backdoor. They had to spend hours every day doing these things. When I wrote that if these costs were reduced income would shoot up, even the most stalwart defenders of the old regime could not handle the challenge. The level of transaction costs were so high at that time, things often did not make sense. This was clear enough, but it took time and many articles to convince people that transaction costs could not be reduced unless the system was changed. I should take credit for that.

Change the system to what? This time, it was more difficult to do the convincing. The first point made in my 1979 paper, that market pricing is the only economic criterion that entails zero rent dissipation, was not difficult for people who had to stand in line for hours to comprehend, but the proposition that the use of market price is uniquely associated with private property was difficult for comrades to swallow. The word 'private' did not bear a single respectable connotation in Chinese culture at that time, and 'private property' was in strict contravention with the official stance of maintaining a socialist or communist state.

It was here that Coase's idea on the delineation of rights worked magic, especially since I as the scientific sales person knew that the same product can be sold with new packaging. When I took the Friedmans to meet the General Secretary of the Chinese Communist Party in the fall of 1988, Mr. Zhao lost no time in elaborating to

Milton the importance of delineation of rights. This dialogue is on record, and it is in print in a number of places. I take credit for selling Coasian economics to the General Secretary. Today on Baidu, the popular Chinese Internet search engine, the "Coase Theorem" appears more than 100,000 times in translation.

What turned out to be crucial is the idea of separating ownership rights from use rights. I was able to draw on many case-examples. At that time, all land in Hong Kong was owned by the (British) Crown, and a private owner of Crown land merely held a long land lease. As a student at UCLA, I bought a small Fiat on borrowed money. I was the registered owner and the bank the legal owner, but my use of the automobile was essentially unaffected by this separation of rights. In Coase's analysis of the delineation of rights, illustrated in terms of beautiful examples in his 1960 paper, I did not see private ownership rights being important in the allocation and use of resources.[10] The issue cropped up when I turned my attention to the so-called responsibility contract, which emerged in China in early 1983. I saw that in the (logical) limit, this would

---

[10] R. H. Coase, "The Problem of Social Cost," *Journal of Law and Economics* (October 1960). In an earlier and equally important paper, Coase wrote: "What does not seem to have been understood is that what is being allocated by the FCC, or, if there were a market, what would be sold, is the right to use a piece of equipment to transmit signals in a particular way. Once the question is looked at in this way, it is unnecessary to think in terms of ownership of frequencies or the ether". Coase, "The Federal Communications Commission," *Journal of Law and Economics* (October 1959), p. 33.

amount to a contract granting the private use of resources without private title. The development of the responsibility contract is central in this paper, so I will defer a more detailed discussion to a later section.

I pass on to Beijing, *circa* August 2006. Zhou Qiren showed me two books of mine, the collections of essays *The Future of China* (1985) and *On China Again* (1986).[11] Both were originally Hong Kong publications, but photographed and reprinted, with the fly-leaf bearing a stamp that says: For Internal Reading Only. The books were listed as internal or 'secret' reading materials for Beijing comrades, and I have never been so happy to see my books pirated (reportedly 2000 copies each). The influence of Coase is clear and pervasive throughout these two collections of papers.

III. A General Concept of Contracts [12]

Armen Alchian advanced the thesis that competition is implied in any society where there is scarcity, and the

---

[11] 张五常，《中国的前途》与《再论中国》，二者皆再版多次，目前由花千树出版。

[12] On July 31, 2002, Milton Friedman's 90th birthday, I wrote in Chinese on "The General Theory of Contracts," which appeared in a chapter entitled "Contract Theory and the Nature of the Firm."（张五常，《制度的选择》，第五章。）From May 24 to August 9, 2007, I published eleven articles discussing "The Missing Link in Economics."（张五常，《经济学的缺环》与《从安排角度看经济缺环》，后者分十篇。《壹周刊》）This second series of articles was written to prepare myself for the present paper dedicated to Coase. In my view, Section III, when combined with the above articles, yields a complete general theory of contracts.

rules which determine winners or losers can be interpreted as property rights. As Armen's student and inspired by China's experience, I have tried to understand the world from a modified angle. In my view, competition for the use of scarce resources must be restrained for social survival, because rent dissipation under unrestrained competition would result in starvation for all. These restraints can assume a variety of forms or different structures of rights, which then define the institutional nature of the economic system.

Rights structures restraining competition are of four broad types, and they generally co-exist in any society. First is the delineation of rights in terms of property, or private property rights. Second is the delineation of rights in terms of hierarchical ranking, or the comrade-seniority system which prevailed under China's previous regime.[13] Third is to restrain competition through regulation. Finally, competition may be restrained by cus-

---

[13] In a different way, hierarchical ranking is also observed in firms in a capitalistic economy. However, the ranking of comrades in a communist system differs in important aspects with the ranking of personnel in a private firm, with the former being closer to the ranking system of a government-funded enterprise such as a public hospital or a public university. In so far as rankings go, the main point of departure from capitalistic firms is that, under communist China, a citizen did not have the right of not joining and had no right to change jobs without government approval. Freedom to choose jobs would bring about the collapse of the comrade-ranking system. When this began to emerge in the Pearl River basin in late 1983, I immediately wrote that economic reform in China had reached the point of no return. Up north, this freedom of choice did not occur until around 1992, after Deng Xiaoping toured the south in the spring of that year.

toms or religion.

Because restraining competition implies mutually-agreed actions, implicit or explicit, voluntary or involuntary, it implies the existence of contracts. The latter need not be market contracts using market prices to transfer rights. I noted in 1982 that a country's constitution is a contract.[14] Private property rights, hierarchical rankings, regulations, customs and religion — all are in my view contractual arrangements of different types.

The broad concept of contracts introduced here is essential. We may in principle classify one type of contracts as intended for the delineation of rights for the purpose of restraining competition, and another type as intended for the transfer of rights, or market contracts using market prices (though the use of market prices is also a way to restrain competition).[15] Difficulties arise because these two types of contracts are not always easy to separate, and in China the two are frequently interwoven. We shall come to this interesting arrangement later.

I have been led by my efforts to understand China to see social interaction in terms of contractual relationships. When I was in Guangzhou in 1979, I was struck

---

[14] Cheung, *Will China Go Capitalist?* (London 1982), Hobart Paper 84, Section II.

[15] Price is a constraint which restrains competition. As Adam Smith puts it in *Wealth of Nations*: "Give me that which I want, and you shall have this which you want......" (Cannan edition, p. 18). A market price is implied.

by the meticulous detailing of rank in different occupations. A certain rank would entitle a comrade to share an automobile, or to an egg every other day, or to the right to buy fish without having to stand in line. These phenomena were thought provoking. My first explanation was that since people are born unequal, in a "property-less" state where everybody is equally "property-less", human rights must be unequal in order to produce social equilibrium. It took me two years to see the deeper truth: The hierarchical rankings adopted in China are contractual restraints essential to reduce rent dissipation under competition, in a situation where the delineation of rights in terms of property is absent.

The important implication here is that economic reform in China involves a shift from a system of rights in terms of hierarchy to a system of rights in terms of property, or a change from one type of contractual arrangement for restraining competition to another type. This, I profess, is the true explanation of what has happened these 30-odd years. The fact that the Chinese managed to succeed without social upheaval may be regarded as miraculous, and as we shall see, the key to success is that they used a contract sitting in between, known as the responsibility contract. The true miracle is not only that they manage to do it, but the system they end up with.

While we are on the level of general theory, let me point out that restraining competition in resource use is costly, and these costs are somewhat misleadingly called transaction costs. I have emphasized over many years that different types of transaction costs can only be separated at the margin, so that testable implications can be obtained by specifying marginal changes in these costs. I have emphasized also that it is not essential to measure transaction costs in (real) dollars and cents, because it is sufficient to measure in terms of our ability to rank transaction costs under different observable situations. No easy task, but it can be done, and I have obtained on numerous occasions predictions or explanation based on specifying observable changes in transaction costs in this sense. You may quarrel with my explanation of why better seats are underpriced,[16] but over the years the accuracy of my predictions of events unfolding in China have earned such high marks that they cannot just be the results of gazing at a crystal ball.

The impossibility of separating different types of transaction costs except at the margin has forced me to broaden the concept to include all costs that do not exist in a Robinson Crusoe economy. As a result, transaction costs often exist in situations where market transactions do not exist. I prefer to use the term institution costs, or costs that exist only in a society. It is my contention that transaction/institution costs arise mainly from restraining competition in the use of scarce resources, or, in my broadened notion of contractual arrangements discussed earlier, from the

---

[16] Steven N. S. Cheung, "Why Are Better Seats 'Underpriced'?" *Economic Inquiry* (1997), pp. 512-522.

requirement of using contracts to restrain competition. The upshot is that so long as competition exists, transaction/institution costs must also exist. In other words, to speak of a society without these costs entails a contradiction in terms.

In 1982, I said that if there were no transaction/institution costs there would be no market. Commenting on the Coase Theorem, I wrote:

> If all transaction costs, broadly defined, were *truly* zero, it would have to be accepted that consumer preferences would be revealed without cost. Auctioneers and monitors would provide free all the services of gathering and collating information; workers and other factors of production would be directed freely to produce in perfect accord with consumer preference; and each consumer would receive goods and services in conformity with his preferences. The total income received by each worker (consumer), as determined costlessly by an arbitrator, would equal his marginal productivity plus a share of the rents of all resources according to any of a number of criteria costlessly agreed upon. By such reasoning the Coase result can be obtained without a market price.[17]

That the market exists because transaction/institution costs are not zero is a view consistent with Coase's classic analysis of the firm, and my early work on the

---

[17] Cheung, *Will China Go Capitalist? op. cit.*, Section III.

choice of contractual arrangements.[18] It follows almost tautologically that markets emerge to reduce transaction costs. However, unlike explaining theater-ticket pricing or the choice of buffet-dinner arrangements, the interpretation of which requires only the specification of certain marginal changes in transaction/institution costs, to interpret complex and involved economic systems or changes in such systems entails a far higher level of difficulty.

My difficulty, which lasted for nearly 20 years, was the result of a mental block. I did not know what kind of transaction/institution costs should be introduced to interpret the existence of private property rights and the market. The broad view I have assumed indicates that these costs are everywhere, and there is no room to add anymore. Then, one night in 2001, I saw the light: We have to deduct, not to add, these costs to obtain the solution.

I then recalled a two-page paper written by Anthony Bottomley, published in 1963.[19] The author argued that pastures in Tripolitania were highly suitable for lucrative almond growing, and yet because of common ownership

---

[18] Coase, "The Nature of the Firm," *op. cit.*; Cheung, "Transaction Costs, Risk Aversion, and the Choice of Contractual Arrangements," *Journal of Law and Economics* (April 1969), pp. 23-42.

[19] Bottomley, "The Effects of Common Ownership of Land Upon Resource Allocation in Tripolitania," *Land Economics* (February 1963).

the land was used for cattle herding.[20] I have always been doubtful that there have ever existed valuable resources subjected to unrestrained common exploitation, but assuming this to be true, dissipation of land rent is implied. What then, would be the transaction/institution costs incurred in the use of the land for common herding in Tripolitania? The answer is the land rents dissipated! In my 1974 article on price control, I argued the dissipation of rent is a transaction cost.[21] In the Tripolitania example the same conclusion is more difficult to draw, but on two counts the land rents dissipated would indeed be transaction/institution costs. First, rent dissipation does not exist in a one-man economy; second, cost is the highest-valued option forgone — in this case the land rents of almond tree cultivation forgone. By definition, the transaction/institution costs of converting pastures to almond cultivation, must, in total, not be less than the rent dissipated, for otherwise the conversion would have occurred. The implication followed is that if we are able to identify specific changes in these costs, then institutional change could be predicted. This is precisely what I did in 1981, when predicting that China would go "capitalist".

It is clear from the above observations that if private

---

[20] In Cheung, "The Structure of a Contract......" *op. cit.*, I noted in addition "that the cost of policing investment in a tree, perennially 'attached' to the common land, is high, whereas cattle are driven home at night."

[21] Cheung, "A Theory of Price Control," *op. cit.*

property in land exists in Tripolitania and almond trees are grown, three results would follow. First, land rents would rise and transaction/institution costs would fall — this fall represents a deduction, and in our example it is the former partially replacing the latter. Second, the type of transaction/institution costs would change, although these costs will never reach zero. Finally, under our broad notion of using contractual arrangements to restrain competition, one type of contracts is replaced by another type. This latter is in my view the true meaning of institutional change.

The above approach may seem new and unfamiliar even to people working on neo-institutional economics, but it is essential to understanding economic reform in China during the past 30 years. In particular, the knowledge I have gained on transaction/institution costs and on contractual arrangements are mainly the fruits of learning from the experience of China.

It is unfortunate that institutional change or changes in contractual arrangements do not always reduce transaction/institution costs or increase rent. Adam Smith's view that land-tenure arrangements evolved to improve efficiency is not always correct.[22] Disastrous arrangements have cropped up on many occasions during the 20th century alone, and I sometimes harbor the thought that mankind may one day eliminate themselves by their

---

[22] See Cheung, *The Theory of Share Tenancy* (Chicago: University of Chicago Press, 1969), pp. 32-34.

own doing in this direction. It is extremely difficult to advance an economic theory of massive self destruction based on the postulate of individual optimization, although I have attempted to do so on several occasions elsewhere.[23] *The Dark Side of the Force*, as my teacher Jack Hirshleifer entitled one of his books, may well explain the popularity of game theory in the profession. I myself do not subscribe to that approach, because I believe that economic explanation requires above all the specification of observable changes in constraints.

Fortunately, for China's economic reforms, the dark side of the force has yet to play a significant role. Whatever the future holds, at long last a great and ancient civilization is emerging from a long, dark economic tunnel. As I said, this paper attempts to answer the question: What has China done right to produce the spectacular performance we all observe?

IV. Evolution of the Responsibility Contract

Let me emphasize again: The central issue of China's economic reform involved the conversion from a system of delineating rights via comrade-ranking to a system of delineating rights in terms of property. This is the same as saying the methods used to restrain competition were changed. Or using the broad concept of contracts dis-

---

[23] 张五常，《从全球暖化说人类灭亡》，二〇〇七年二月二十二日；《世界末日好文章》，二〇〇七年三月八日。二文皆于《壹周刊》发表。

cussed earlier, the contractual arrangements used to restrain behavior were changed. The contracts in question are not the usual market contracts we know, but they are contracts nonetheless as they stipulate what individuals may or may not do when they compete in society.

How can a transformation from a system of comrade-ranking of rights to a system of property ranking of rights be implemented? Ideological and political considerations aside, a great difficulty cropped up in the early 1980s in that such a change implied a reshuffling of income not acceptable to the status quo. My hope at the time was that the initial transformation would produce such a sharp jump in total income that individuals experiencing a drop in ranking would be compensated by substantial absolute increases. A jump in income did occur, as several localities in southern China experienced 50% or more growth rates in 1983. Still, the transformation met with opposition from the earlier privileged. In April 1985 I wrote proposing to pay them off and buy back the comrade-ranking rights.[24] Somewhat quixotic and clearly difficult, this suggestion surprisingly received some support in Beijing. However, no such action ever took place.

A different compensation scheme emerged: corruption. Corruption became widespread around mid-1984.

---

[24] 张五常,《官商的天堂》,一九八五年四月十二日发表于《信报》,其后转刊于《中国的前途》。

At first I was relieved, because corruption was replacing the earlier back-door transactions.[25] This was a clear sign that the comrade-ranking system was collapsing. However, when Beijing announced in 1985 that they would introduce controls by product classification, I immediately wrote that China was on "the road to India", arguing that if rights to corrupt were to be delineated in terms of regulations, the reform process would come to a halt.[26] With this warning, supporting voices from Beijing became strong. Controls by product classification were abandoned.

I disagree with suggestions that regulated corruption would be good for economic development. Experience in China does not support this view. The fact that corruption is negatively correlated with growth falsifies the view that it contributes to growth. However, if there is any credit in corruption, then I may say in the case of China it helped to pay off the privileged and reduce their resistance to reform. I also disagree with the view that corruption is everywhere in China today. It is still popular, but compared with the 1980s and the early 1990s,

---

[25] "Back-door transactions" refer to the buying and selling of favoritism. Favoritist transactions do not imply corruption, but are based on rights implicitly granted to comrades of different ranks. There is no violation of the law. 见张五常，《贪污的后患》，一九八五年一月三十日发表于《信报》，其后转刊于《中国的前途》。

[26] See Steven N. S. Cheung, "A Simplistic General Equilibrium Theory of Corruption," *Contemporary Economic Policy* (July 1996).

corruption has subsided a good deal. I know enough government officials who take pride in their work to negate the view that corruption is everywhere. Anti-corruption policies have been strong since 1993, and, as we shall see, these efforts were assisted by locality competition. My view is that compared with other Asian countries, the level of corruption in China is currently on the low side.

When transforming from one system of contractual delineation of rights to another, China was fortunate that the process was assisted at the early stage by a market contract bearing a market price. Known as the responsibility contract, it became immediately successful when applied to the use of land in agriculture. In 1986 I wrote:

> The so-called "responsibility contract," if reduced to its simplest and therefore most perfect form, is equivalent to the granting of private property rights via a state lease of land. Duration of the lease may be for any number of years or, in principle, may be perpetual. Ownership is not relinquished by the state, but the rights to use the land and to obtain income are exclusively assigned to the lessee. The right to transfer, or to sell, the leased resource may take the form of subletting. Various dues exacted by the state may be lumped together in the form of a fixed rent, and since this rent is paid to the state, it becomes a property tax. If indeed a perpetual lease is assigned, then the holding becomes fee simple, and if the right is freely transferable, then the lease is held in fee simple absolute — or private property

in its perfect form![27]

Trying to understand the development of this contract, I had the good fortune that my colleague C.H. Chai generously made available to me detailed source material collected over the years (no small effort, that), and this enabled me to publish a 1984 paper on the responsibility contract in agriculture.[28] It all began in 1958 with the rapid introduction of communes throughout the country. Massive starvation followed, and memory of this painful experience lingered for twenty years. To mitigate the effects, a number of modifications to the commune system were introduced. First was the work-point system; then came production teams; then there was a shift from large teams to small teams; and then in 1978 responsibility contracts began to emerge.

"Responsibility" may not be a completely accurate translation. In Chinese, it means "guarantee what I want and you can do what you want." At first the responsibility contract was applied to production teams, but in 1981 it was extended to households with the specification of target outputs. By 1983, the terms changed to households guaranteeing the delivery of fixed amounts and keeping the residual. The official extractions were several and complicated, but they were simplified over time, until in 2005 agricultural taxation was abolished. The

---

[27] Steven N. S. Cheung, "China in Transition: Where Is She Heading Now?" *Contemporary Policy Issues* (October 1986).

[28] 张五常，《从"大锅饭"到"大包干"》，一九八四年十一月十五日发表于《信报》，其后转刊于《中国的前途》。

government maintained the right to purchase agricultural products at controlled prices until the early 1990s.

There is no question that the responsibility contract met with great success in agriculture. Land was fairly evenly distributed among households, mostly by head count, and transfers of the right to land use for agricultural purposes were soon allowed through reassignment of responsibility contracts. However, enormous difficulties emerged when responsibility contracts were introduced in industry. In industrial production physical assets depreciate and may get stolen, and state workers could not be discharged under existing laws. Trying to get to the bottom of the difficulties, in 1985 the City of Shenzhen assigned three young men to assist my research. Sample contracts in manufacturing were promptly produced upon request. They took me to visit factories. The results from all this effort were meager. The changes were too rapid, and with contractual terms changing so frequently I was unable to produce analytically interesting generalizations.

It was at this juncture, around 1985, that I strongly urged the separation of use rights and ownership rights, hoping that as a result state-owned enterprises can be more readily privatized.[29] In 1986, I was invited to Beijing Steel to look at its responsibility arrangements. I stayed in the dormitory for several nights and gave a

---

[29] Elaborations of this view can be found in Sections II and III of my Chinese work *On China Again*《再论中国》, which contains nine articles written between May 1986 and March 1987.

talk. Sixteen years later, on 22 April 2002, I had the honor of being invited to deliver a lecture at the Party School of the Central Committee of the Communist Party of China. The dean of its business school picked me up at the airport, and on the way he told me he was in the audience at Beijing Steel. He said that afterwards everyone was warned not to believe my suggestion that ownership rights and use rights should separate, and that the responsibility contract with delineated use rights should be pushed to the limit. "Heroes think alike" — so the Chinese saying goes — not much later, separation of use rights and ownership rights became a pillar of what Deng Xiaoping was to call "Chinese Style Socialism."

The gentleman from the Party School quietly remarked that back in 1986 he could not imagine he would ever own a computer, but now he could afford to buy a new one every other year. I was deeply moved to hear this, for old timers like us who knew what the country was like not that long ago, what has happened is more of a miracle than can be appreciated by younger people who know little of China's past. It was a long drive to the Party School, and I came to realize that the old comrade was proud of the China miracle, and that there must have been many like him who stuck to their guns when the ship was taking water.

V. The Manifestation of the Responsibility Contracts and the Rise of the Competing Xians

The responsibility contract was a success in agriculture, though it took some years to modify and simplify the complicated arrangement to yield the present form of transferable land leases. In the process, the authorities gradually relinquished direct controls in favor of delineation of use rights. By the early 1990s price control was dropped, and in 2005 agricultural taxation was abolished, thus rendering the responsibility contract in agriculture the equivalent of a long land lease free of taxation. Nonetheless, it is still formally a responsibility contract. The selling of agricultural land, which in reality is a transfer of the land lease, is still called "changing responsibility."

Applying the responsibility contract to industry was more of a problem. When I began to study the matter in the mid-1980s, the main difficulty lay in depreciable industrial assets. Responsibilities over maintenance and reinvestment led to frequent controversy between the authorities and state enterprises. I proposed several solutions, such as the issuance of transferable stocks.[30] This scheme was adopted in the late 1990s, but only for profitable state enterprises enjoying protected monopoly status. As for the numerous losing concerns, their physical assets were mostly depreciated to zero value by the early 1990s. In fact, by that time the authorities had difficulty giving away loss-making state-owned factories.

Different times, different problems. Beginning in the

---

[30] See the sources in n. 29 above and my Chinese work *The Economic Revolution of China*《中国的经济革命》(1993), reissued with additional chapters in April 2002（花千树出版有限公司）.

1990s, the sticking point with state enterprises no longer concerned assets — there was hardly any value left to depreciate — but that state employees cannot be discharged under law. Nevertheless, large-scale privatization of loss-making state enterprises was successfully carried out around the turn of the century, effectively assisted by a substantial rise in land prices. We shall explain what happened later.

An idea of great value was salvaged from the disappointing experience of the responsibility contract in the industrial sector. Around 1984, a layer-by-layer responsibility arrangement emerged. In essence this was subcontracting, and we know in industry how the "subs" may go down a number of layers in a chain. If we must single out one key development in China's economic reform, then my choice is that beginning from the late 1980s responsibility contracts in agriculture was combined with the layer-by-layer responsibility arrangements in industry. This is a truly significant achievement, because the combination was applied neither to individual farms nor individual state-owned enterprises, but to entities defined by geographic boundaries. In my view, this is the central feature of the economic system of China today.

For someone following the day-to-day development of this system he might find it very complex, but when the changes finally settle down and one is able to put the pieces together, the system is seen to be straightforward and rational. What happened has not been tried anywhere before. Although none of the parts are new, the way they are put together is original and effective. During the early application of responsibility contract combinations to localities, the arrangements differed in different places and changes were frequent, until around 1994 the common features of the whole became identifiable. I came to appreciate that there was something truly special about the system when I looked into the development of Kunshan in 1997. The intensity of competition among localities then was something I had never seen before. When deflation ended around 2000, locality competition became so dynamic that I did not fully decipher the workings until the end of 2004. It is true that in varying degrees, competition among localities also exists in other countries, but as we shall see, both in nature and in intensity, what is observed in China has no equal elsewhere.

Although many of the people involved were very capable, I do not believe that the system of China now in place is the result of brilliant individual efforts. The system as it stands today is rather the result of economic pressures, with many mouths to feed and the rising tide was roaring. To handle the situation, the guiding principle followed was not the popularly quoted saying of Deng Xiaoping — "feel the stones when crossing the river," but that the man of few words said: "Give it a try, and then take a look."

Let me begin the description of the locality-competing system by clearing up a matter of terminology. Each and every locality of course has a proper name, but their common names — whether city or town — are often confusing. Some of the common names are different because they were coined at different times, and today some localities are specially treated because they report directly to Beijing. I prefer my way of classifying localities, which is generally endorsed by official friends.

It is instructive to view China as consisting of seven layers, all geographically determined, with a lower layer falling inside the confines of the layer above. The top layer is the country, then comes the provinces, the cities, the xians, the towns, the villages, and finally the households. These seven layers are linked vertically by responsibility contracts, but horizontally there are no contractual linkages. Competition therefore occurs horizontally but not vertically. Entities bearing similar responsibilities compete against one other, within the same layer.

The intensity of locality competition varies positively with economic power assigned to each layer. Today, economic power by and large rests in the xians. The chief economic power does not rest in the villages or towns or cities or provinces or even Beijing but in the xians, for the reason that xians possess the right to decide and allocate the use of land. The central government in Beijing (and to a lesser extent the provincial authorities) reserve the right to define and enforce general guidelines regarding land use and other general economic and political matters. They also possess the right to shift the geographic boundaries of localities, to fire or reshuffle local officials, and to reallocate funds to assist localities under certain conditions.

The right to decide and allocate land use is the key issue in a developing country. Without land there would be nothing to develop, and if land is used efficiently all other considerations become secondary. If under competition land rents are rising, the economy is growing. Technology change and the accumulation of physical and human capital are no doubt important, and the country is marching forward in these areas — right now, the growth rate of private R&D expenditure in China is the highest in the world. But technology and investment would be of little effect when people do not have enough to eat. Take care of land use, lift the masses from starvation, and then the economy can take off with the support of saving, investment and technological change.

Efficiency in land use can be realized at different levels. Other things the same and given clearly delineated use rights, how high a level is attained depends on the intensity of competition. Individuals compete, households compete, firms compete — these represent all the forms of competition traditionally analyzed in economics. In the case of China, we may add that localities within the same layer compete, and because economic power rest mainly with the xians, competition at this level is the most intense. Adding one more layer of competition is, in my view, the chief new idea in the answer to the China question.

A xian is often translated as "county". That is not correct. In China, cities are very large. An average city contains 8.6 xians. At the end of 2006, the official count was 2,860 xians or the equivalents in the whole country, so that there were this number of entities which possess a high degree of autonomy regarding land use and related economic matters. The average area of the xian is about 3,000 square kilometers with a large variance. Since population density is low in western China, the xians there tend to be very large in area. In the populous east of the country, a xian is typically in the neighborhood of 1,000 square kilometers in size. I estimate the average population per xian to be 450,000, but here again the variance is large.[31]

The question remains — the central question remains: Why is competition so intense among xians? Is it not true that in other countries there are different layers of localities too? Exactly what are the fundamental elements in the contractual structure of the system of China that generates intense competition, and which in turn sustains economic growth at the spectacular rates we have been observing?

VI. The Sharecropping Nature of the Xian System

Economic reform in China can be divided into phases. The first dates from around 1980 to Deng Xiaoping's

---

[31] The granting of economic power to xians via responsibility contracts has given rise to an interesting debate during the past few years. Should cities in China be abolished? The pros argue that while economic power rests with the xians, politically city officials are ranked higher, so that unavoidable conflict would emerge which interfere the operation of the system. This is a complicated issue which I did not tackle during my research. Beginning fiscal year 2007, xians report financial matters directly to provincial governments, skipping the cities. In other political or administrative matters, a city is still ranked higher than a xian.

retirement in 1992. This phase involves mainly the delineation of rights in terms of property to replace the earlier practice of comrade ranking, with the high point being reached on December 1, 1987 when Shenzhen auctioned land for the first time in the country. This involved selling a private long lease to use land for a specific purpose without private ownership. City officials told me they were following my advice: I had earlier suggested that selling land was just about the only way funds can be obtained to develop the city, and that they should allow private developers to exploit private expertise.[32]

During this first phase, economic development was concentrated in the Pearl River basin, in the south of the country. This was a relatively neglected and underrated region during the earlier regime, with few large state enterprises or state-protected monopolies. Businessmen and investors from Hong Kong led the way, bringing in capital, technology, and management skills. Compared to the Yangtze River basin where powerful state enterprises barred competition, down in the south days and sometimes hours were all that it took to obtain a private business license.

The impact of the market began to be felt in the Yangtze River basin around 1993. Surprisingly, in only eight or nine years this area overtook the south in just

---

[32] In June 1986, I published an article discussing three advantages of selling land. Shengzhen officials liked that article and invited me to a meeting in the spring of 1987. 张五常，《出售土地一举三得》，一九八六年六月二十五日于《信报》发表，其后转刊于《再论中国》。

about all the vital economic statistics. This marked the second phase of economic reform in China, when Zhu Rongji was in charge of the economy. The period 1993 - 2000 included some trying times, beginning with runaway inflation, massive corruption, the collapse of the RMB, followed by severe restrictions on borrowing and spending, crackdown on corruption, and finally by deflation and the collapse of the real-estate market. Yet it was in the midst of these difficulties that the Yangtze River basin exploded in growth, with effects which extended all the way into the mid-western part of the country. One may cite a number of reasons for this miraculous development, but in my view the key factor was that the xian-competing system finally emerged in a well-defined form, and that it began to deliver results.

The odds were against the Yangtze River basin overtaking the Pearl River basin under the economic climate described above,[33] and yet this was what happened. The

---

[33] In the fall of 1988, I took the Friedmans to tour the Yangtze River basin. Milton was happy to see street vendors doing business on muddy roads, and told the General Secretary (whom we later met in Beijing) that street vendors would have to bribe to obtain a license. Suzhou officials obligingly showed us their famous town-and-village enterprises, which were embarrassing. During dinner, a vice mayor of Suzhou argued with Milton on the superiority of state enterprises. In the fall of 1993, I again took the Friedmans to China. One main street in Shanghai was fully lit at night, and we all applauded when our bus passed a shop owned by traveling companion Jimmy Lai. The Friedmans stopped briefly in Shanghai in 1998, and Milton could hardly believe what he saw.

reason is that the xian system worked better in the Yangtze River basin, because down south private enterprises were already established under earlier contractual arrangements. Factories were scattered hither-thither, untidy and dirty, but business interests were significantly vested. In other words, in the south there was a lack of the flexibility in land use necessary for xians to compete effectively. Not that the southern xians do not compete, but they did not possess the flexibility to juggle land use which their northern counterparts enjoyed. This experience also taught us that the belief that dispensing with government planning and relying on the market is always more efficient is wrong. World-class industrial

---

Two episodes of the Friedmans' China visits should go on record. First, I taught Milton a lesson in Chinese economics. In Shanghai, 1988, walking in the street and hungry, I saw a dumplings vendor and pulled out my wallet, but found out money was not good enough: food coupons were also required. A passer-by saw that I was arguing with the dumpling man, and gave me a small stack of food coupons. I was delighted, and Milton asked why I was so happy. I said, "The gentleman gave me these coupons free of charge. Can you imagine food coupons worth nothing? This city is going to explode!" It did. A second episode is that Milton lost a debate! In Chengdu, 1993, the governor of Sichuan province received us. Milton tried to teach the governor about the proper way to reform, saying that to cut the tail off a mouse, don't do it inch by inch: To reduce pain the whole tail should be cut off all at once. The governor responded: "My dear professor, our mouse has so many tails we do not know which one to cut first." Milton could not respond. Sadly, that governor is no longer with us. A courageous man noted for his bold criticisms, it is said that he lost support from Beijing at the end.

villages cropped up in the Yangtze River basin, with beautiful landscaping and all the modern facilities, and they were routinely planned by xian officials. They plan, however, for the market! The officials know that good things sell better. They also know that they are likely to be sacked if what they plan does not sell.

There is a formula for distributing income between xians and the higher authorities that is important in promoting competition. Very briefly, at the early stage fixed amounts were paid to the higher authorities. This often led to conflict, as some localities felt that they were being exploited just because they did well. Sharing arrangements were then introduced, with quarrels occurring again because the rates were not the same among localities.

This brings us to an important development in 1994. From then until now, investors in a locality or xian are subject to a 17% value-added tax which is uniform throughout the country. The xian is entitled to one-quarter of this, or 4.25% of the value added in production. Alternatively, a small private enterprise may pay 4% to 6% business tax (depending on the nature of business). Profit tax is on top, but this does not concern us here. For the purposes of our discussion we may also ignore the business tax, which one has to pay even when losing money. The value-added tax yields by far the highest revenue, and it is this tax that xian officials are most concerned about. Let us therefore concentrate on the 17% tax on that part of output value over and above the cost of raw materials and other deductibles.

The question is whether this take of 17% is a tax, or a rent? My view is that it is rent and not tax, for two reasons. First, whenever an investor uses land or real property to generate income then he is required to pay the tax. Second, this tax would have to be paid as long as income is generated, regardless of profit or loss by the accounting measure.

In 1986, I observed:

> In ancient China, as in medieval Europe, no distinction existed between the meanings of "rent" and "tax." A feudal lord who collected rent became a collector of tax when he assumed the role of a "government" in providing services such as justice and protection.[34]

It may seem trivial to quibble over what is tax and what is rent, except in the paradigm of economics tax maximization is routinely criticized, while rent maximization is often endorsed. The truth of the matter is that for the efficient use of land rent would have to be charged, no matter by the landlord or by the government. How the proceeds are spent is a separate matter. It is my contention that since the xians are competing, the maximization of rent is consistent with efficiency provided all land is used. This does not mean there is nothing left over for the investors. Their expected income net of the rental tax must be sufficient to cover interest cost, and if the economy grows because of their investment, their

---

[34] Cheung, "China in Transition......," *op. cit.*

income may well exceed what had been anticipated. In fact, most investors have been doing very well under the xian system, particularly since 2000. In other words, with the economy growing and land rents rising, there are implied increases in income which fall into the hands of investors, workers and peasants. Judging from the shifts in the relative prices in favor of agricultural products since 2003, these implied increases are very substantial indeed.

The uniform 17% level selected for the value-added tax was reached after many rounds of negotiation with the different localities. It is clearly share rent and hence a clear case of sharecropping between the xians and investors on the one hand and between the xians and the upper levels on the other hand. There was an analytical conundrum which took me months to resolve. I wrote *The Theory of Share Tenancy* 40 years ago, and one of the main points of departure from tradition was that I allowed the sharing percentage to vary to obtain efficiency results. It was clear from the evidence in Asian agriculture that sharing percentages varied significantly according to land grades and localities. But now the value-added tax, a share rent, is the same throughout the country. How can that lead to efficiency? If not, why would China have accelerated so much in growth under the sharing arrangement?

One night I recalled a footnote of Marshall which I read as a graduate student, and jumped out of bed to find it. Marshall argued that share rent is less efficient than fixed rent, but he added a footnote:

> If the [share rent] landlord controls the amount [of capital] freely and in his own interest, and can bargain with his tenant as to the amount of labor he applies, it can be proved geometrically that he will so adjust it as to force the tenant to cultivate the land just as intensively as he would under the English tenure [fixed rent], and his share will then be the same as under it.[35]

To this I responded in my sharecropping work:

> Marshall provided no geometric proof, and it is an interesting conjecture whether he would have altered this footnote had he done so. This conjecture is interesting because the results he conceived are correct only in certain special cases, but as a matter of generality they are incorrect. They are incorrect because Marshall did not allow the rental percentage to vary.[36]

Based on Marshall's footnote and my comment, and assuming the xian as the landlord, I asked myself what amount of 'capital' can the xian provide to guarantee an efficient solution when the sharing percentage is held fixed and uniform. The answer, which I discovered around the end of 2004, is that the land price charged by the xians (to investors as sharecroppers) can actually be negative! Taking land to be the capital contributed

---

[35] Alfred Marshall, *Principles of Economics* (8th ed., 1920: London; Macmillan Co. 1956), p. 536, note 2.

[36] Cheung, *The Theory of Share Tenancy, op. cit.*, p. 45.

by the landlord, the possibility of using a negative land price means the landlord is offering infinite opportunities for adjustment, under which the equi-marginal condition required for efficiency can always be attained as long as the uniform sharing is within a reasonable range.

By a negative land price, I mean that when an investor comes to a xian to consider investment and production, the xian may not only give improved land to the investor free of charge, they may even build the facilities *gratis*, or allow the investor a rebate over a number of years out of the value-added tax the xian is entitled to. Of course, not all xians are worth investing in, as there is no point building a factory in the hilly wilderness. Social returns aside, the guideline of how negative a land price can be offered is a return high enough to cover the interest forgone in the xian's efforts to obtain and improve land for industrial or commercial usage. We will return to this question in the next section.

Beijing's prohibition on land prices going negative, imposed in 2006 for some xians, suggests that they did not understand the working of the implicit sharecropping system. But it may not be so. There is the problem that China's population would be concentrated in the popular regions, to the detriment of a more even distribution which is more desirable in the long run. I wrote about the issue, but could offer no solution. There are matters for which market prices are not available to guide decisions, as Coase and I have expounded in our work on the firm, and errors can only be discovered *ex-post*.

VII. The Sharing Formula and Its Effects

One evening in 2005, the head of a xian from far away called, saying he happened to be in the neighborhood and wanted to drop in for a visit. He came, took off his shoes, laid on the sofa, closed his eyes for some minutes, and then asked, "Professor, may I have a glass of wine?" Of course he may.

I knew what must have happened. Xian officials like this friend run all over the country soliciting investment. Whenever a business-inviting conference is held in a certain city, the word would get around and officials from countless xians would arrive. It is not uncommon these days that xian officials dine at business occasions several times in one evening.

A xian with a mere 300,000 in population would often employ 500 investment solicitors. In 2005 a xian in Anhui province held a beauty contest, selecting the most beautiful, charming and persuasive ladies to head the teams. Criticized all over the country, the head of that xian fought back: "Beauty is an asset, why not use it?"

Want a business license? The xian will assign someone to do the walking and talking for you. Want a building permit? They will give you one with a money-back guarantee. Unhappy about that dirty creek passing through the site? They may offer to build a small lake for you. They will help you find architects, find builders, and coming to the production phase, they will help you recruit workers for a reasonable fee. Yes, xians have worker-recruiting teams, which do the hiring for clients. They sell their cheap electricity, sell their parks and entertainment, sell their easy transportation, sell their water supply, sell their glorious history, and sell even how good-looking their girls are — no exaggeration!

Competition among localities of a level comparable to that among xians in China is unheard of. Why is this so? One contributing factor is the sharing formula. Let us explain this formula before turning to other factors in the next section.

As we have seen, investors coming to a xian would have to pay 17% in value-added tax. Of this the xian is entitled to a cut of 25%, or 4.25% of valued-added. From the proceeds from land sales (if positive) 75% goes to the xian and 25% to higher levels. This latter percentage is not uniform for all xians: the better a xian is located the lower will be its share of income from land sales. Of the xian officials I talked to, none of them cared how the higher levels divide their take.

Land costs are substantial. These consist of two parts. First peasants must be paid to give up their land. Using a 5% rate of interest, I estimated in 2006 that such payments come to about 3 - 5 times the discounted market rental of the land when used for farming. Quarrels between xian officials and peasants occasionally occurred, but far less frequently than reported in the press. It is true that some officials take secret cuts in between, and that a xian short of funds may owe the peasants for a long period of time.

The costs of developing or improving agricultural land for industrial or business use are even more substantial. In 2006, these costs were in the neighborhood of RMB 60,000 per *mu* (660 square meters), about twice the compensation to peasants. Improvements include building roads, putting in power, water, gas, and sewers, cables for telephones, television and computers, street lighting, and landscaping. These improvements are made before the land is sold. Today, even in lower level areas, the quality of new industrial real estate offered by the xians is higher than what I was familiar with in the State of Washington. At the top level, like those in the Suzhou industrial village, it is the best I have ever seen. Chinese peasants are superb in planting things — they often transplant trees over fifty years old — and you cannot beat what Arthur Lewis would say is an "unlimited supply" of them working for landscaping at US$ 5.00 each for one long day.[37]

---

[37] This was the figure in 2004, in the middle of the fastest rise in peasant income in the history of China. It was a daily wage, and by 2007 the figure had risen to about US$8.50. The amount varies in different areas, and I took rough averages when I toured villages in China on photography trips. From 2003 to 2005, I produced enough photographs to publish seven books, so what I say about the livelihood of peasants in China, though deviates sharply from all other reports, is based on prolonged and intensive investigations conducted on site, in exactly the same way as I investigated apples and bees in the State of Washington in 1972. See Steven N. S. Cheung, "The Fable of the Bees: An Economic Investigation," *Journal of Law and Economics* (April 1973), pp. 11-33.

I did some rough calculations in 2006, using data from a xian of moderately above-average performance, to arrive the following results. Assuming that an industrial site is built to a plot ratio of 0.8 and a factory of typical labor intensity, the xian's 4.25% cut of the value-added would come to 12% of the total cost of acquiring the agricultural land and improving it to a good industrial site. This did not include administrative costs, but the figures suggest that the xian could indeed afford to give away the site freely and subsidize the investor a little.

There is no question that within a xian and in the sale of virtually identical industrial sites at the same time, the land price may vary greatly. Except for occasional favoritism that leads to scandals, price discrimination is not implied. Xian officials are selective of the type of investors they want. What they are going after is not only the value-added tax, but also the image and reputation an investor would bring, compatibility with existing economic activity, and so on. It is not unusual that when an investor's project is believed to be a big draw for the locality, the negative land price would go so far down that the xian's cut in the value-added tax would not cover interest on the cost of land.

Xian officials may sometimes be corrupt, but over the years I have never met a stupid one. They know that equalizing marginal social returns from similar sites is the way to maximize income for the xian and for themselves, and if the prices of similar sites are equal there is no way they can achieve that. They also know that it is very difficult to make accurate judgments in investment, and therefore they send researchers all over the country visiting successful xians. In numerous discussions with xian officials I have been impressed by their general knowledge of things, and know they are forever concerned with matters such as complementarity, drawing power, transportation, electricity, water, entertainment, and so on. I am not saying that xian officials are never corrupt, but the truth is that I have never met an investor who did not believe in exploiting special connections. Yes, xian officials are world-class in convincing each and every investor that he or she is special!

Let me repeat that while the rate of value-added tax and the division of that tax is uniform throughout the country, the other percentages are not. In particular, the sharing of the proceeds from land sales is not uniform, and less popular xians would receive higher shares to partially cover land costs. Additional mention must be made of award figures in the formula. Based strictly on investment money deposited in local banks, in one xian I know that officials receive 1.5 - 2% that amount, if the investment is from outside the country. For investors from inside China, the award is 1%. These are essentially commissions paid by the xian. For the xian in question the award rate in earlier years was 5%, which gradually fell as the xian grew. In one hot spot, the award rate is 0.05%. The rate is negotiable, in the way that commissions on property transactions in China are negotiable. Most xian officials I talked to felt that award rates were adequate to keep them running.

VIII. Economic Interpretation of the Xian Phenomenon

The intensity of competition among xians is remarkable. It is submitted to be the chief reason why China was able to sustain rapid growth during some very difficult times in the 1990s. Vietnam copied China's system nearly verbatim beginning from around 2004 — some say tipped off by my writings — and their economy, too, has taken off. It is not difficult to copy this system, provided that a country is not burdened with vested interests at local levels, and that it possesses an organization like the Chinese Communist Party to force things through. My view is that countries like North Korea and Cuba would have a good chance of success if they want to try.

Not difficult to copy, but very difficult to explain. It is difficult to explain why the system works so well. It took me only one evening to crack open the riddle of sharecropping, but three long years to decipher the China code. The difficulty stems from the fact that what we have here is a complex system of contracts, the like of which has never been seen. Its evolution has been rapid, and in the process different localities adopted different arrangements before things finally settled into a comprehensible pattern. It takes time to see the essential links and elements, and by the time I thought I have distilled the beer from the froth some key pieces were still missing. I have learned a great deal following the economic reforms in China. My understanding of contracts and transaction/institution costs had been elevated to a level which enabled me to locate the missing pieces with a general theory, and then put the pieces together to form a picture that makes sense.

Perhaps I should begin by relating an episode in the spring of 1969, when Coase and I were in a conference on fisheries in Vancouver. Someone remarked that if ocean fishery is privatized, because the fish swim for long distances the granting of monopoly is essential, therefore monopoly pricing in fishery would prevail. I instantly responded: "If I alone own all the agricultural land on earth, I would have to rent them out to numerous peasants to farm; the peasants will compete, and therefore agricultural products must have competitive prices."

Now Beijing is the largest landlord in the world, holding the title to all land under the Chinese sky. The authorities let the land out for a variety of use with fifty year leases, and in 2007 it was declared that all leases would be automatically renewed upon expiry, subject to the proviso that the government may see fit to take back land subject to compensation. The authorities have accepted the principle that all use rights must be delineated as exclusive. They also knew that to do so comprehensively, they have to allow the delineated use rights to go all the way down to each and every household. To maintain control of an orderly downward transmission of economic forces and knowing that responsibility contracts worked, the layer-by-layer responsibility arrangements emerged. For an outsider studying the rules and regulations from documents of the different layers, there is little chance he could figure out that a chain of responsibility contracts is implied. These documents are actually revised and evolved versions of the earlier responsibility contracts.

Different layers are vertically chained, but horizontally there is no linkage. This is one reason why units within the same layer compete against one another, and because economic power rests mainly in the xians, at that layer competition is the most intense. Adding fuel to the fire, the delineation of rights applies everywhere. The geographic boundaries defining a xian are clear, and the rights and responsibilities of xian officials are assigned in such a way and with such clarity that there is no question that xians are effectively business firms of the first order. Business firms of the same nature compete, and this is another reason for the intense competition among xians.

Still adding more fuel to the fire, xian officials are rewarded according to performance. No doubt politicking and corruption are present, but these activities, too, can be expected in large corporations in advanced market economies. Other than the formula of awards described earlier, xian officials are entitled to business expenses rather generously, depending on how much money the xian makes. Each individual is allowed to buy one living quarter at construction cost, and is subject to promotion based on performance. There is a '56-year-old hypothesis' in circulation: With salaries so low and awards inadequate in some xians, and with the retirement age being 60, by the age of 56 officials not having enough savings are inclined to be corrupt. Some officials, however, told me that competent individuals are on demand from outside businesses, because managing a xian is in fact managing a business.

The adoption of value-added taxation in 1994 was another addition of fuel to the fire. In essence, it is sharecropping. As noted in my early work, under sharecropping the landlord cares a lot more about the performance of tenants than when there is a fixed rent, because his income depends on tenant performance.[38] A vivid example to illustrate the intensity of competition among the xians is that of shopping malls. A xian may be viewed as a large shopping center, under the umbrella of one corporation. Tenants renting shop spaces in the center are the equivalent of investors in a xian. The tenant pays a fixed minimum rent (the equivalent of an investor paying a fixed land price), a share rent on top (the equivalent of value-added tax), and we all know the shopping center owner is careful in selecting tenants and tries to accommodate tenants in many ways because of share contracting. And, like shopping centers offering special deals to anchor stores, xians offer special deals to investors who they consider to be big draws. If a whole country is filled with such shopping centers, doing similar business but with the entities being separate, the intensity of competition among them would be very strong indeed.

The xian system does more to encourage competition

---

[38] Cheung, *The Theory of Share Tenancy*, *op. cit.*, pp. 72-79.

than the hypothetical shopping centers. Xians are held responsible to the layers above. Thus these upper layers not only encourage competition — they enforce it! After all, the upper layers are entitled to a 75% cut of value-added tax. It is here the layer-by-layer responsibility arrangement intensifies competition among xians.

Let us return to the nature of the responsibility system to comprehend better the intense competition among xians. During the evolution of that system, the delineation of use rights, and hence private property rights, is woven into market contracts. As the Coase Theorem implies, the use of the market is in two steps. The first is the delineation of private property rights, which in my view is itself a contract restraining competition for scarce resources. The second step comes with the market proper, where the rights to use resources or to the outputs produced are exchanged under the form of price-bearing contracts.

The responsibility system rests on a different arrangement. It combines the delineation of private use rights and market transactions into one contract. An investor in a xian often signs a contract only several pages long, stating land size, location and price, what he can do and what he must do, and by what time various duties must be discharged on both sides. The deed to the land, however, will not be issued until some months after money from the investor is lodged in a local bank. This signed market contract is transferable, but for future sale of the land or for mortgage purposes, the land deed issued later helps a great deal.

The question in my view is why the weaving of property rights into a market contract is so significant in encouraging competition, as compared to the two-stage process envisaged under the Coase Theorem. The answer is that with the weaving-in arrangement the investor is obliged to perform. Other than paying money, the investor has to discharge the contractual stipulations to secure the right to use the land. In other words, price aside, responsibility contracts are meant to be awarded to deserving winners. Errors in judgment of course occur, and investors playing tricks are not unusual, as some may just build a fence around the property and do nothing more. When land prices are falling xian officials may look sideways, but when the economy picks up they will move to reclaim the property per contractual stipulations. There was plenty of screaming from investors around 2000, when sharply-fallen land prices began to turn around. However, investors who performed as stipulated were all smiling.

The weaving-in arrangement as described is not unique to China. As Coase rightly points out, lease and employment contracts in many countries often exhibit similar features, and I have pointed to the similarity to contractual arrangements found in shopping centers. I have also noted that none of the parts in the xian system is new. What is new and important is the way the parts are put together through the manifestation of the responsibility contracts: Namely, use rights are granted in exchange for performance, and that this basic principle applies everywhere. In particular, in the industrial sector the contractual arrangements between the state and private entities, via weaving-in and with sharecropping and the layer-by-layer chaining, is an awesome display of economic forces at work, at a time when more than one billion people were poor but the leaders were courageous enough and intelligent enough to follow the principle of "give it a try and then take a look."

The rights structure implied by chained responsibility contracts is reminiscent of the constitution of a country, except that arrangements in China are more flexible in that the terms are negotiable, and in general they are far more market oriented than under any constitution I know. In February 2004, I published a long article "It is Not Yet Time to Revise the Constitution," trying to halt the constitutional revision in progress at that time.[39] My point is that the economic system of China is so important that Beijing should study the nature of the system, pinpoint the key elements, and introduce them into the constitution. Beijing did not heed this advice, and the subsequent revised constitution has little bearing on the economic system's rights structure. Apparently Beijing did not fully appreciate that they have done something right, beautiful, and brilliant.

Four implications of significance are obtained from our study of the Chinese economic experience. First, to the importance of the market and private property in advancing life and livelihood, we must add the question

---

[39] 张五常，《还不是修宪的时候》，二〇〇四年二月十六日，《信报》。

of how contracts are arranged and structured to form an economic system. We have shown that the economic system of China involves a far-reaching but delicate structure of contracts the like of which has not been seen, and the competition among xians which this contractual arrangement promotes is, in my view, the key to answering the "China question". Of course, as scientists we cannot rule out the possibility that there may be other contractual arrangements that would work better, but are as yet untried. As things stand at the turn of the century, and given the country's relatively poor natural resource endowment, I submit that the economic system of China is the most effective engine of growth in the history of mankind.

Second, how individuals and institutions are constrained matters in the choice of contractual structure that defines the economic system. The xian-based system works very well for China, a country with a huge population and exiguous natural resources but blessed with an intelligent people capable of working long and hard. For a country more richly endowed, adopting China's economic system may well bear less fruit.

Third, the speed of economic growth depends a great deal on the contractual structure which defines the economic system. We have seen that xian officials give priority to investors who promise to perform faster, and they themselves routinely add a hefty shove to the push. The sharing formula dictates that what the officials earn is directly and positively related to the rate of growth. Therefore, it has been a mistake on the part of Beijing that when they saw the economy growing at more than 8 or 9 per cent a year, far higher than in the outside world, anxious thoughts emerged regarding "over-heating" and polices were introduced to cool things down. My close observation of China for 30 years suggests that economic fluctuations there are attributable to changes in policy, while not one trace of business cycles of the endogenous type described in the western world has been observed.

Finally, I do not believe the evolution of China's economic system could have progressed to a situation of near-miracle without the government or the Communist Party playing a significant role. As I unhappily indicated in the "Epilogue," this golden age seems to have lasted only 29 years. Make it or break it, the government was, and is, important in China's economic system. It is a sad omen for economics that most, if not all, of the stupid policies recently adopted in China were conceived in the abstract by returning Ph.D.s in the subject.

IX. Side Effects of Xian Competition

One has to be careful reading Chinese newspaper reports on economic policies these days. The articles are not lying, but they tend to mislead because the writers generally do not understand the economic system. Since xians are given substantial autonomous decision-making powers on economic matters, sometimes what is announced by Beijing as an intended policy is not followed. Minimum wages have been introduced at different dates and vary greatly among xians, and some xians merely announce that there is one but choose not to enforce it. When Beijing announced that 70% of apartments must be built to no more than 90 square meters, some localities announced one or two such projects when selling land, while others acted as if nothing has happened. Newspaper headlines say that one outsider cannot buy more than one living quarters: Shenzhen currently enforces this policy, but Shanghai says they have not heard of it.[40]

This does not mean that Beijing is not in control. They are in control, but local officials know what type of announcement is for real and what type is meant to test the waters. Local officials have their way of evaluating the seriousness of the documents handed down to them. Requests from Beijing for local opinions regarding policies are routine, and adopted policies may be quietly dropped without announcement. Some villages have democratic voting, some do not, and those who do introduced voting at greatly different times.

I surmise that this seemingly chaotic picture is not really chaos, but it is the result of a combination of the autonomous powers given to localities and varying decisions on the part of the localities to adopt policies. In particular, a decision to adopt policies for window dressing is subject to considerations as to whether the xian

---

[40] By November 2007 this rule applied to Shanghai also, but different parts of that very large city have different ways to get around it. The rule has therefore never been enforced in Shanghai. In Shenzhen the rule was enforced for a while, then an outsider who wanted additional living quarters could buy a way for about US$4,000, and then the property market fell and the government looked sideways.

would gain in competition. A xian would have to attract more investors to increase value-added tax — indeed to survive — and the officials know the adoption of bad policies will drive them away. If Beijing really meant to enforce a policy, the xians will accept, but if the policy is contrary to locality interests, they will complain. The complaints are often effective if the number is large enough.

It is difficult to demolish the rights structure of the xian system, and this is a good reason to support the optimistic view that the rapid growth can be sustained for many years to come. The problem lies in matters in which the localities have no say: The monetary system, exchange controls, foreign policy, freedom of speech and religion, state-monitored education and healthcare, communications, and the activities of large state monopolies.

I am concerned that Beijing does not seem to have an adequate comprehension of the workings of the economic system, for there are indications that they are trying to tamper with it.[41] My view is that with some gentle fine tuning, the system will be solid and firm. As I remarked

---

[41] On 1 January 2007, Beijing imposed two items on the xians. First, compensations paid to peasants to obtain land were substantially increased. This is a judgment call. Second, all land sales for construction purposes must go through auction. In principle this latter would run counter to the workings of the xian system, but there is a way out. A xian would make a land auction project specific, and with obscure advertising and short lead time, a successfully negotiated investor is usually the auction winner.

in my long article of February 2004, in idealized form the layer-by-layer chaining of responsibility contracts with sharing arrangements possesses the merit that, if the delineated rights of one member in the chain are infringed upon, all members in that chain must in some degree share the cost of that infringement.

Because of locality or xian competition, joint-venture contracts with foreigners were developed into a special form of patent licensing, with royalty payments remittable to foreign banks free of exchange controls. I have investigated patent licenses for some years and fully understand the difficulty of their enforcement, but taking the form of a joint-venture contract with a foreign director on site to monitor performance, enforcement costs would be sharply reduced. This is one reason why foreign investors flock to China today. Zhou Yan miraculously got hold of a number of samples of these joint-venture contracts, and earned a doctorate in a good dissertation analyzing them. I have arranged to have her deliver a *precis* in this conference, so I will say no more.

Because of xian competition, concentration of industries by type in particular locations is very pronounced. Chinese products are flooding the world market, but little is known in the outside world of the degree of locality concentration and specialization of industrial production. The ceramics industry of Foshan is a classic example, and I have arranged Li Junhui to write a paper on the subject for this conference, as she is teaching at the University of Foshan.

Because of xian competition, privatization of state

enterprises has been pressed to proceed faster. Around the turn of the century, a rise in land prices greatly assisted privatization. With higher land prices, local governments could afford to pay off state employees and remove the major obstacle to private purchase. Buyers of the state enterprises would sell properties located in prime areas and move the factories to where land is cheaper. The City of Changsha may have broken the world record in the speed of state enterprise privatization. I have arranged for their vice-mayor, Liu Xiaoming, who was in charge, to deliver a paper detailing what happened.

Xian competition has also been a force to reduce corruption. Other things equal, only uninformed investors will put money in a xian noted for corruption. Experienced investors know bribing is a cost, and in earlier days factory owners down south routinely penciled in such costs when quoting prices to buyers. Not all corruption is gone, but at the xian level it is very much reduced, particularly when compared to the early 1990s. Officials I talked to concur that competition among xians have helped to bring this about.

Finally, it is my view that the great flexibility of contracting observed all over China these past ten or fifteen years — other than the chain of responsibility contracts as discussed above — is also the result of competition among xians. It was this flexible choice of contracts that helped to save China from recession in the second half of the 1990s.

One question remains: There will come a time when

the conversion of land use from agriculture to industry and commerce would hit very strong diminishing returns — perhaps ten years from now. Will the intense competition among xians observed today vanish? My answer is that some weakening of competition will occur. However, given the nature of the xian system, fresh directions would doubtlessly be found in which to compete. The most likely and profitable candidate is competition in terms of technology. For this reason I have advised my Beijing friends to hold firm to the value-added tax, because technological progress is the most effective way to increase value added.

X. The Monetary System of China and the Rise of the RMB

Zhu Rongji is a brilliant man. Though seated in several different offices, the general consensus is that he was the man in charge of the Chinese economy from July 1993 to March 2003. Zhu had every appearance of a planner, a dictator, a market skeptic, and I criticized him for his handling of inflation in 1995. Later, I openly apologized in writing and on television: He was right; I was wrong.

We cannot evaluate a reformer based on what he says or even on what he does. The performance can only be evaluated on the basis of results. By this measure, Zhu deserves full marks. Appearing to want power, yet during his tenure central economic power was significantly reduced. Critical of the market, yet during his tenure domestic markets became so free that they were inspiring even to dyed-in-the-wool neoclassical economists. You may accuse the market of selling fakes, but the sharp improvements in product quality rival those of Japan during a similar stage of development, and market contracts, both for goods and services and for workers, exhibit a range of choice seldom seen elsewhere.

In 1993, inflation in China was accelerating and the RMB was diving. I published an article on May 21, saying that there was no point to control the money supply, because it cannot be done.[42] The problem was that banks in China were payroll offices, and that people in power could 'borrow' on demand. I therefore proposed that the People's Bank should assume the duties of a central bank and not engage in business transactions. Even more importantly, I argued that the power demand for money must go.

Zhu Rongji took charge of the People's Bank on July 1, 1993 and stayed in that post for only two years, but he created the basic framework of China's monetary system and monitored its performance until retiring from the premiership in March 2003. In 1995, he converted the People's Bank into a central bank of the classic type. What he did to curb inflation was direct restrictions on borrowing and spending, with the RMB anchored to the US dollar. I was doubtful of the merits of such restric-

---

[42] 张五常，《权力引起的通货膨胀》，一九九三年五月二十一日，《壹周刊》，转刊于张五常，《二十一世纪看中国的经济革命》，花千树出版，一七五至一七九页。

tions, but then this may have been the only way to cut off the power demand for money. Influenced by Friedman, I objected to the pegged rate.

When Hong Kong's Financial Secretary decided to adopt the currency board system and peg the Hong Kong dollar to the US dollar in 1983, I was involved in the discussions. Charles Goodhart argued that the Hong Kong dollar must be anchored, and Friedman supported the currency board. What about the RMB? In the late 1980s it was showing signs of difficulties, and by early 1990s its exchange value began to collapse. I consulted Milton on a number of occasions, and he was extremely generous with his time whenever issues involving China cropped up.

Milton's view was that a country the size of China could not use the currency board. He said that my suggestion of anchoring the RMB to a basket of commodities would work in principle, but the cost would be high. His choice was that China go to fiat money, control the money supply tightly, and let the exchange rate float.

In July 1997, soon after the Asian financial crisis struck, a group of economists from Beijing asked to meet me in Shenzhen. They were deeply concerned about what would happen. During the discussion I suddenly turned bullish, because I began to realize that Zhu was right. In three short years he brought inflation from over 20% to zero, and given sharply rising product quality at that time deflation must be implied. I inferred then that the Asian financial crisis was a consequence of the sudden and sharp strengthening of the RMB. In one way or another most countries in Asia, including China, tied their currencies to the US dollar at that time, so when inflation came to a halt in China, under international competition the small boats tied to the dollar broke loose because their currencies became overvalued.[43]

About a year later, I began to appreciate the Zhu system even more. His method may be interpreted as anchoring the RMB to a tradable index, using the dollar as a proxy, and the issuance of the RMB was guided by the inflows of foreign direct investment. He guarded that index with care. Inspired by Zhu, I came to the view that a currency may anchor itself to a tradable index of a basket of commodities, without having the real commodities in store, provided that the monetary authority possesses foreign reserves for occasional intervention and more importantly that monetary policy is not used to correct problems in the real economy. If money is kept to monetary phenomena, then anchoring the exchange value to a tradable index would not be difficult to attain and sustain.

---

[43] I did not publish this explanation at the time in fear it might trigger further disturbance in the currency market. When I finally did so on April 27, 2006 in a Chinese article entitled "The Story of the Iron Prime Minister," a Beijing friend who was expert on the crisis was stunned and told me that my explanation must be right. He and his colleagues were fanatically seeking an explanation for the crisis at that time, but in retrospect whatever they came up has proved false. 见张五常,《铁总理的故事》, 二〇〇六年四月二十七日发表于《壹周刊》。

It was the flexibility of market contracts that helped to save China from recession in the latter part of the 1990s. Deflation exceeded 3% even ignoring sharp improvements in product quality, and property prices dropped two-thirds or more. However, unemployment stayed around 4%, and the growth rate around 8%. Bonus contracts and piece-rate contracts, overwhelmingly used in industries, provided automatic downward adjustments in real wages.[44] Furthermore, to protect his eight-percent goal, Zhu freed the market completely, pushed hard for the privatization of state enterprises, lifted restrictions to allow workers to freely 'float' around the country, and speeded up the dissemination of economic decisions. Zhu might have started out as a market skeptic, but he must have turned believer before stepping down.

To return to money matters in China. In a lecture delivered at Tianjin's Nankai University in 2002, I argued that the RMB was the strongest currency in the world — at that time the black market rate was still below the official rate.[45] Then in March 2003, in an article commenting on Zhu's retirement, I said the RMB was so strong that within two years western countries will pressure China to appreciate — the black market

---

[44] Bonus contracts provide automatic downward adjustment in wages. Piece rates are equally flexible because they are often renegotiated when new orders from buyers arrive. 见张五常，《制度的选择》，第四章，第六节，二〇〇二年花千树出版。

[45] 张五常，《以中国青年为本位的金融制度》，二〇〇二年六月二十日发表于《壹周刊》。

rate was about on par with the official rate then.[46] These assessments of currency strength in terms of interactions between official and black rates were based on discussions with Milton in 1993 and my understanding of underground currency dealings over the years. Beijing, of course, was fully aware of these activities.

Outside pressures to appreciate the RMB did come, not two years later, but in about four months. I have stood firm against any significant appreciation of the RMB. The reason is that to improve the livelihood of the peasants, they must be encouraged to move to the industrial sector. In no way could China's economic reform be regarded to be successful, unless the peasant's standard of living is lifted to a level on par with city workers. For centuries, the tale of Chinese peasants has been blood, toil, tears, and sweat. For the first time in memory the peasant is seeing a glimmer of light, but a substantially appreciating RMB will extinguish that hope.

I told Milton in Stockholm in 1991, on the occasion of Coase's Nobel Prize, that the world would soon see an introduction of one to two billion cheap workers into international trade, and the structure of the global economy would be very different in 20 years. That competition has arrived, and my concern for China is that wage rates in the country, though low, are now substantially higher than places like India and Vietnam. I am delight-

---

[46] 张五常，《令人羡慕的困境——朱镕基退休有感》，二〇〇三年三月十一日发表于《苹果日报》。

ed to see these countries, too, are developing strongly, for the simple reason that the richer they are, the more money China will make trading with them. However, appreciating the RMB in effect amounts to offering a handicap. How could Chinese peasants gain a higher standard of living with a sharply rising RMB, when even today many of them have not seen a real plane flying?

There are numerous factories in China which I have called order-takers. They hold no patent rights and no brand names, but only execute orders to produce to given samples or designs. Whenever a purchaser wants a certain product, he would send out requests for samples and pricing, sometimes to several countries. My view, supported by hard fact, is that Chinese peasants trying industrial work generally begin in order-taking factories, and then move up the ladder with acquired skills and knowledge. I am grateful to Bob Mundell who, too, has spoken out loud on many occasions against significant appreciation of the RMB.

It would be easy to relieve the market pressure to appreciate the RMB. Instead of foolishly suppressing demand for money — which the authorities are doing at the time of writing — they should drop exchange controls and let the RMB out to freely trade in the international market. Downward and upward pressures on a currency are not symmetrical. A currency facing downward pressure is a headache, but one facing upward pressure is not badly off. Letting the RMB out as proposed above makes money for the country, and since China is already flooded with foreign reserves it would be easy to buy the RMB back if need be. Any concern about inflation can be removed by anchoring the RMB to a basket of commodities.

Inspired by Zhu's monetary system, I suggested in 2003 and repeated it several times, that the RMB should be anchored to a basket of commodities, or rather to the price index of such a basket. No commodities need be held in storage by the monetary authorities. The authorities simply guarantee the RMB holder that a given amount would purchase the specified basket in specified markets.

This tradable index is easily adjustable, which means the domestic price level would be easily adjustable. The selection of commodities and the assignment of weights require careful consideration, but if done properly inflation will no longer be a matter of concern. The idea of anchoring a currency to a basket of commodities was discussed with Milton years ago, and it is consistent with the views of Mundell. Zhu's experience suggests the costs would be low in practice, because a currency may successfully anchor itself to a tradable commodity price index and no actual commodities need be held by the monetary authorities.

Beijing considered my proposed monetary system carefully, which in reality is the Zhu system modified. The modification involves taking one step sideways to avoid confrontation with other nations, by saying: "Here we are back to the old commodity standard, except that we go by a tradable index and hold no commodities in reserve. This is how we value our currency, and against all other currencies exchange rates are freely floating." Of course, to guard against inflation it would be far better to anchor a currency to a tradable index of real things than to paper currencies.

I am not disturbed that the central bank has not accepted my suggestions, but what they have done over the past two or three years are matters of genuine concern. Other than what have been mentioned, my impression is that they want to go to fiat money. In this case, monetary policy sooner or later would have to enter. This will sharply increase the power of the monetary authorities to intervene in economic activity, which would in due course increase the risk of undermining the xian system.

Let me repeat an important point made earlier. The rights structure of competing xians cannot be easily demolished. Any unwarranted policy which infringes on the xians' interests and in which they have a say, I do not worry about. For example, I do not worry about domestic price controls or rent controls, and if they are introduced I put my money on that they would not be enforced, or if enforced the controls would be lifted before long. But I do worry about are policies in which the xians have no say. In this regard, monetary matters are at the top of my trouble list.

XI. Concluding Remarks

I have concentrated on what China has done right to

produce an economic miracle, thinking I would introduce a few negative remarks to balance things out at the end. But I find myself reluctant to do so. This is the 30th anniversary of the beginning of economic reform, and Chinese tradition teaches that we do not throw mud on someone's face on his or her birthday. And it is not just someone. It is a civilization once so rich and so deep that some of the fine pottery and jade carvings produced 5,000 years ago cannot be replicated even today. This heritage I am proud of, and those who study Chinese history and culture will concur that it is a source of pride for mankind. A renaissance of the Chinese heritage is occurring right now.

Beijing has a great deal to be proud of. Criticize the authorities in detail if you want, but they have done so much to relieve poverty, on such a massive scale and with such speed, that there cannot be any parallel in history. I surmise that such an accomplishment would never be repeated — anywhere, anytime.

I have stood firm on the merits of private property and the market for more than 40 years. However, I have never objected to the existence of the Communist Party of China. From day one I opposed reform through the democratic voting process. In no uncertain terms I told a group of old comrades during our first encounter in Beijing in 1983: "You messed the country up; you fix it for me." We became good friends. Sadly, many of them are no longer around. They have delivered far more than I anticipated. In the middle of the night I sometimes wonder how some of them would react if they could live long enough to see the China of today.

The Communist Party of China has done a marvelous job! Political parties have problems, all kinds of problems. How is it possible to properly organize party activities and enforce party rules when the membership is 80 millions strong? It is mind-boggling.

The Party led the way and directed the action. But the main reason for success is the Chinese people, hardy, intelligent, and resilient, who can take a huge amount of suffering today when they see opportunities opening up tomorrow. I am not going on to praise the Chinese people, but I have never seen individuals working so hard for so little under such miserable conditions — and still smile. In 2004, while taking photos in the wilderness, my wife had a conversation with a woman working in the field. This woman said she had a pay day every so often, when someone called and bused her to the industrial district to do landscaping. Leaving home before dawn and returning in darkness, surviving on a loaf of bread and a bottle of water, she earned US$7 a day. I saw her smiling and asked why she was so happy. She said livelihood had improved because her expertise of planting trees was for the first time in her life in demand from outsiders, and that her daughter had just graduated from college with a good job at US$200 a month. It is individuals like that woman, millions and millions of them, who have built up the China of today.

I published my first Chinese article in 1979, but writing in earnest did not begin until the fall of 1983. Chinese officials and business executives in their prime

CONCLUDING REMARKS

today were college students then. Many of them read my writings, and as an old man now I get free meals everywhere I go. It has been a pleasure wining and dining with them and at the same time obtaining first-hand information to support the writing of this paper. I here thank them all, with deep sincerity, and thank them again for the roles they have played in pushing their country to see the dawn of light.

Popular reports that say Chinese officials are routinely corrupt are simply not true. Many are highly intelligent and dedicated. An ethos of competition exists among officials and businessmen which reminds me of my student days at UCLA in the early 1960s. Within each group they know or have heard of who is who, assess each others' ability, and play the competitive game of performance ranking. It is as if they have no purpose in mind except to see who could climb higher.

The xian official who came to visit and asked for a glass of wine is one example. He worked so hard for so small a salary — about US$300 a month — that I wondered what drove the man. Would it be corruption money? Promotion? Prestige? Very subtly I tried to feel him out. After a while he knew what I was going after, and said: "My dear professor, I just want to do something for the country." If and when the environment is sufficiently inspiring, we may see many such people around.

I return to China's miracle. Other than the economic system itself, I rank two developments as truly miraculous. First is the explosive growth in the Yangtze River basin that stretched all the way into the mid-west, beginning around 1993. This took place during a period which began with the collapse of the RMB, 20% inflation followed by 3% deflation, and a fall in property prices by two-third or more. Second is the explosive rise in peasant income beginning around 2000, when deflation came to an end. I estimate that, from 2000 to 2007, the per-capita income of peasants increased about 20% per year. Three out of four peasants of working age have floated to industrial and commercial employment. If this trend continues, it will take no more than ten years for the average income of peasants to catch up with the medium income group living in the cities. Trends, of course, cannot be counted on, but if the trend continues, I estimate that in twenty more years China's economic status would amount to ten Japans.

In closing, I must pay tribute to the man I once criticized. He is Zhu Rongji. As my teacher Armen Alchian often reminded me: it is results, not motivation, which measure success. The two noted miracles, which I rank above all others, both occurred during Zhu's tenure as China's economic navigator. Future history will not forget this man.

*   *   *

An Unhappy Epilogue

The above was written in August 2007. Except for some unfortunate tinkering with Zhu Rongji's monetary system, I felt that there was every reason to celebrate the

30th anniversary of economic reform in China. I did not pay attention to the New Labor Contract Law at that time. This law was passed on 29 June 2007 to become effective on 1 January 2008. The xians were not consulted before the decision.

I received a copy of the law in October 2007, and with one glance at its 98 articles I knew it would be a disaster. But I was in the middle of a series of articles on inflation, and could not respond to the new development until December. When my first critical article appeared on December 13, supporting voices were strong.[47] However, on 27 January 2008, six government organizations held a conference at the University of Beijing to argue against my views. I have written a total of eleven articles commenting on the new labor law, mostly elaborating relationships between the firm and the market which Beijing apparently did not understand. These articles have not had much effect: After subsequent meetings held in Beijing in March 2008, it was clear the authorities are adamant to push this new law into effect.

Essentially what the new law says is that labor contracts are no longer free. They must follow stringent guidelines determined by the government. Over-time pay is doubled, room-and-board provided by the employer cannot be deducted from wages, all contracts must be in writing, holidays and benefits of workers must be such and such, labor unions are encouraged, firing procedures

---

[47] 张五常，《新劳动法的困扰》，二〇〇七年十二月十三日发表于《壹周刊》。

are modified — all for the benefits of workers, and a tenure system similar to that found in US universities is introduced: a worker will automatically be granted a contract to retirement, if he or she has been employed by the same firm for ten years.

Although the timing matches perfectly, I would not venture to say that China's stock market crashed as the result of the new labor law and the serious intent to enforce it as expressed in the March Beijing meetings. As Newton remarked, only God understands the behavior of stock markets.[48] Nor would I venture to say that the sharp fall in exports during January and February 2008, notably in toys and garments, was the result of the labor law. (The snowstorms which hit the country were the worst within memory.) However, I can say that some 120 factories owned by Koreans in a town in Shandong province quietly closed during the Chinese New Year holidays, so when the workers returned they found everything shut and no one around. The new law hurts old establishments more, so that thousands of factories closed down in traditional industrial districts, with multiplier effects going down the supply chain. Workers were sacked left and right. Many restaurants in the old industrial districts went bankrupt. There were protests in the streets.

---

[48] After losing a fortune in the stock market, Newton said, "I can calculate the motions of heavenly bodies, but not the madness of people." See John Carswell, *The South Sea Bubble* (London: Cresset Press, 1960), pp.131, 199.

Seeing that the industrial outlook has suddenly turned gloomy, a department in Beijing placed the blame on the sub-prime crisis and recession in the United States. But this is negated by the facts: exports of similar items from Vietnam, India, and Pakistan have been increasing. There is no question that the new labor law has triggered a shift in favor of other cheap-labor countries. Lower level industrial investors in China are moving out, especially to places like Vietnam. They will bring their clients along, when the factories now under construction are ready for operation.

It is inconceivable to me that Beijing is not aware of what is happening. The authorities must know. So why? Why did they insist on pushing the new labor law as late as March 2008, when the negative effects were becoming apparent to all and sundry? Except for some lawyers and a tiny fraction of the work force, everybody would lose. The governor of Guangdong succinctly stated that any government policy must consider its effects on workers, employers, and the state, and in his view the new labor law would hurt all three groups. He was apparently not welcome in the March Beijing meeting.

I can see very little special interests that can be promoted by the new labor law. Even the lawyers I talked to opposed it, saying the expected increase in legal business cannot compensate the staffing problems they will have to put up with. Considering the new law is introduced on the 30th anniversary of China's economic reform and the year of the Beijing Olympics, it is truly baffling.

I have three plausible explanations, and most likely it is a combination of all three, although in economic logic things do not add up. The first reason is that Beijing did not know that the incomes of poor peasants and low-level workers have been sharply rising since 2000, at rates which in my view are unmatched in history. However, workers earning less than RMB 1,600 per month do not have to report tax, and floating workers simply do not report, so their incomes are difficult to assess. More important is the fact that registered population in the villages remains large, although many people have floated away. If one divides the observed total income of peasant households with the registered population, an artificially low per-capita income is obtained.

In January 2004, two Chinese authors published a book which won international acclaim. This book reports that Chinese peasants are having a difficult time.[49] A year later, the World Bank reported that the livelihood of Chinese peasants has deteriorated since the country joined the World Trade Organization. Such statements, coming at a time when peasant wealth and welfare was improving at the fastest rate in Chinese history, are irresponsible. Indeed, as recently as 3 March 2008, Justin Lin reported in the aforementioned Beijing meeting that the income distribution in China is becoming more and more unequal and unfair. This was the

---

[49] 陈桂棣与春桃,《中国农民调查》,二〇〇四年一月人民文学出版社。

main issue of his report.⁵⁰ Justin is the man in charge of agricultural policy, so how could he not be aware that Chinese peasants have never had better days than now? How could he not know that in terms of percentage growth the income gap has been closing fast the past several years?

The new labor law is intended to help the poor, but on 17 January 2008 I published an article predicting this law would create a downward kink in the rising income curve for China's poor.⁵¹ This kink is beginning to be obvious now!

A second plausible reason why the new law was introduced is that President Hu has expressed the principle of a scientific approach to development.⁵² No one can object to that, but unfortunately this principle has been interpreted by many to imply an intention to phase out low-tech labor-intensive activities. It should not be forgotten that the economic reform is meant to lift the masses out of poverty, and that for a country with a large population like China, embodied capital-augmenting technological progress requires labor of both high and low productivities competing and supporting from below.

Finally, there is the bad influence of western econom-

---

50 《林毅夫称收入分配不合理越来越明显》，二〇〇八年三月七日《新京报》。

51 张五常，《灾难的先兆——三论新劳动法》，二〇〇八年一月十七日发表于《壹周刊》。

52 胡锦涛提出"科学发展观"。

ics. The so-called efficiency-wage theory, the validity of which is in doubt,[53] has been interpreted by returning Ph.D.s to mean that if workers are paid more they would produce more. I can accept the view that given two groups of identical and homogeneous laborers, the higher-paid group would tend to perform better. This is no more than saying that if a publisher doubles my writing fees, my articles would read better. But at what level would an employer want any given worker to perform? What about the lower-paid group? Why should the minimum payment be decided exogenously by the government?

Returning at last to the main thesis of this paper, one must ask: What about the power of the competing xians? Though they had not been consulted before passing the new labor law, what about their resilience to unwarranted central intervention as I described? At this moment, most xians ignore the new law. However, it will be difficult to resist this time, for three reasons. First, there was a 'soft' old labor law which by and large has not been followed or enforced. The new law draws attention to the old violations. Second, because of Article 14 of the new law (tenure provision), employers and workers are

---

[53] There are some people who believe that the efficiency-wage theory stems from my paper "Why Are Better Seats 'Underpriced'?" (*op. cit.*), but what I meant in this work is not what the new theory says. A critique of the efficiency-wage theory can be found in my Chinese book *The Choice of Institutional Arrangements* (2002), pp. 156-159. 张五常，《制度的选择》，二〇〇二年花千树出版，一五六至一五九页。

forced to look back ten years. Finally, Beijing has proposed to pay workers' legal fees if they wish to sue employers. What a mess!

What would happen if Beijing stands firm on the labor law? Other than what I have described, two outcomes are certain, for we already see them unfolding. The first is that enterprises would seek evasive contractual arrangements, not only with regard to labor but in corporate structure. Whatever happens, ultimately transaction costs would increase with detrimental effects on economic growth. Secondly, producers would increase automation and screen out less productive workers. For the moment, the majority of factories which are closing down are relatively small or 'marginal'. This would create the impression that Beijing has succeeded in promoting technological progress by reducing labor intensity, but what will happen is that technological progress shall be hindered by a weakening of labor support from below.

Beijing authorities today have apparently forgotten the motto of Deng Xiaoping which has served the reform process very well: Give it a try, and then take a look. They should try out the new labor contract law in a few selected xians first, monitor and observe their performance, compare to others without, before deciding what to do.

Because the situation in China is changing fast, I must point out that this epilogue is written on April 8, 2008.

*   *   *

On 9 May 2008, a set of rules for the enforcement of the new Labour Contract Law appeared on the Internet. Comments were solicited from the general public, with 20 May as deadline. Some lawyers began to interpret these rules to be revisions aimed at softening the economic impact of the law. Then came the 12 May Sichuan earthquake. Economic concerns are now in abeyance, as the genii of the Chinese people are pitched against the destructive forces of nature, and the world watches with deep sympathy and increasing admiration the triumph of the will.

Steve, 31 May 2008

中国的经济制度

中国的经济制度

第一节：中国的问题

个人认为，中国的经济改革始于一九八〇。一九七九的秋天，我到离别了多年的广州一行，看不到任何改革的迹象。北京与将来的史学家无疑会选一九七八为改革的起点。这里日期明确：一九七八年十二月二十二日。那天，中国共产党的第十一届三中全会公布了一项极为重要的决定。有了这个日子，罗纳德·科斯策划的这个中国研讨会议就有一个特别的意义：肯定是历史上最伟大的经济改革，今天刚好是三十周年了。

当年的三中全会决定了两件事。一、中国开放推动经济发展；二、邓小平再获授予权力。那时，相信这两项公布的人不多吧。关于经济，类似的豪言壮语曾经表达过。至于邓的复出，这是第三次了。虽然这一次说明他获授予的是最高的权力，但资历比他高而又反对市场经济的同志，大有人在，而一九七八年的中国，资历辈分重要。

有谁知道将会发生什么事？邓可能再下台。

一九七九的夏天，英国的经济事务学社的主编要求我写关于中国的前景。他说撒切尔夫人的办公室对一个学术性的分析有兴趣。那年的秋天我到广州一行，跟着是愈来愈有兴趣地跟进中国的经济发展与改革。一九八一年，我察觉到中国的局限在急速转变，于是为该学社写了一篇足以印成小册子的文章。一九八二发表，《中国会走向资本主义的道路吗？》注一做出了肯定的推断：是的，中国会向市场经济的道路走！延迟了一年才出版，因为不同意的批评者无数。在西雅图最亲密的同事巴泽尔，不同意我的推断，但他认为关于理论那一节真好，不发表很可惜。

于今回顾，我当年的准确推断使朋友与同事惊奇，而我自己惊奇的，是跟着的改革发展速度。差不多三十年持续的高速经济增长，超越了日本的明治维新，而发生于一个那么庞大，人口那么多而又是那么复杂的中国，近于不可置信。还有的是，在这奇迹的发展中，中国要面对贪污，面对一个不合格的司法制度，控制言论与宗教自由，

注一 Institute of Economic Affairs (London: 1982), Hobart Paper 84.

教育与医疗公非公私非私,有外汇管制,有互相矛盾的政策,也据说每年有六万次动乱。除了动乱的统计数字——不知定义为何,不同地区的朋友说他们没有见到任何他们会认为是动乱的——其他上述的负面事项皆属实。

大约二〇〇三年,几位熟知中国的朋友向我投诉国家的多种不是。我回应:"不要告诉我什么不对。我可以在一个星期内写一本厚厚的批评中国的书。然而,在有那么多的不利的困境下,中国的高速增长持续了那么久,历史从来没有出现过。尤其是,不要重复某些人相信的:贪污对经济发展有利。朱镕基的肃贪行动早就把这假说推翻了。中国一定是做了非常对的事才产生了我们见到的经济奇迹。那是什么呢?这才是真正的问题。"

我用一个比喻对这些朋友解释困扰了我好几年的问题。一个跳高的人,专家认为不懂得跳。他走得蹒跚,姿势拙劣。但他能跳八英尺高,是世界纪录。这个人一定是做了些很对的事,比所有以前跳高的做得更对。那是什么?在不同的内容上,这就是中国的问题。

这篇文章要找这问题的答案。长而复杂,因为我有一段历史要叙述,有一个理论要解释。这样，我要专注于中国做对了什么。这里我只能再说，要批评中国我可以写很多本书。

自一九八〇起，中国真是个经济奇迹。米尔顿·弗里德曼曾经高举香港的经济奇迹，因为人口上升了十倍而人均收入还有可观的增长。然而，香港以北的深圳，人均收入的增长比香港还要快，而同样的时间人口上升了四十五倍。举另一个例，我和太太造访绍兴后五年，再回去面目全非。报道说，一些劳工离乡三年，回乡找不到自己的家。有些深在内陆的城市，像旧金山市那样，高楼大厦在夜间灯光闪闪。目前，世界上过半的新升降机是在中国装置的。

今天在中国，高速公路每年建造四千多公里，足以横跨整个美国。九十年代中、后期，世界百分之十七的建筑起重机集中于上海。那时楼价急跌，但午夜还可见到熔焊工人在高高的钢架上操作，仿佛天上的星星。上海在五年间建成的商业楼宇面积，比发展得快的香港的五十年还要多。二〇〇二年，上海的策划者突然大幅减低楼宇建筑的容积率，因为发觉高楼大厦的重量使该市下沉。从南京到上海的四线公路，启用时因为车辆稀少而被批评浪费，但五年后交通堵塞，进账可观，要扩宽为八线了。因为车辆按大小收费，载货超重严重，世界级的公路很快就被轧坏了。整个国家的所有港口都要排队落货。二〇〇五年,地球最长与次长的跨海大桥同时建造,而且是在同一地区。

温州一家造鞋厂雇用十二万员工。该市差不多产出地球上的所有打火机及圣诞灯饰。义乌,十五年前以地摊小贩多而知名,今天每日输出过千个货柜,来自韩国及非洲的购买商人云集该市,使写字楼的租金升穿楼顶。有谁听过几千间店子只卖短袜,不卖其他?这是义乌,那里的批发商场大得我一看就坐下来,因为老人家不容易走那么远。乐从镇有一条马路,两旁满布家具商店,长达十公里。苏州的广大工业园,园艺美观,满是世界级的名牌工厂与世界级的厂房设计,五年间在农地上冒出来。杭州每年游客四千万。该市有一间零销店,出售一个名牌的皮包,每天平均进账八万美元。

我可以不断地继续叙述类似的现象。没有什么意思吧。需要补加的,是浦东的一个故事,即是上海黄浦江之东。一九九三年我带弗里德曼夫妇到那里,见到的只是一行一层高的店子,据说是建造给邓小平看的。米尔顿当然反对这样做,指出政府的发展策划一般失败收场。然而,八年后,我带一位美国建筑设计师到浦东商业区,他目瞪口呆，说那里密集的摩天商厦可能是世界上最好的。上了一课：一个像中国那么大，人口那么多而又发展得那么快的国家，会有很大的空间容许以尝试的方法学习。注二

今天，浦东的商业楼宇还在建造不停，空置着的很多。楼价却在上升。这些看来是互相矛盾的现象只有一个解释：人们在等待。他们下注投资而等待，期望着一旦中国解除外汇管制与金融管制，上海浦东会立刻成为一个有领导地位的金融中心。

统计的数字加不起来。一个从事统计的官方朋友，直言无法前后一贯地把数字组合。二〇〇五年，北京相当大幅地把过往统计的增长率提高，

注二　当一九九七年上海宣布将在浦东建设一个新的国际机场，怀疑的人说旧机场的使用还没有达到饱和点。浦东的新机场一九九九启用，过了不久一条跑道不够。二〇〇五增加了一条跑道，二〇〇八再加一条及一个新的候机处。旧机场现正增建另一条跑道。这样看，上海每隔两年半就增加一条国际机场跑道了。

收费的公路与桥梁有类同的故事，本来亏蚀的没多久就赚钱。一位朋友惋惜卖掉一段公路，因为不久后满是车辆。一家来自台湾的规模不大的方便面生产商，五年后每天产出三千万包。从二〇〇〇到二〇〇六这六个年头，在中国投资的人差不多不能出错。可惜好景不长，到了二〇〇七年底，这乐观的景象不再。

但这调整可没有算进产品与服务的质量是戏剧性地改进了。不止此也,大部分的省份统计的增长率,高于北京对全国的统计,有些高很多。二〇〇六年,广州报道该市的人均收入暴升,但主要是因为他们用产出总值除以户籍人口,忘记了数百万没有户籍的流动人口的产出贡献。没有疑问,二〇〇〇年起农民的生活直线上升,但官方的统计却说他们的增长率低于城市的。他们一定是用了户籍人口算,因为没有谁知道多少农民"流动"去了。我认为三分之一以上的劳动人口在国内流动。不知道这个陷阱,外间的机构几番报道,说中国的基尼系数正在危险地上升。这些报道脱离目标要以英里算。

第二节:思想的冲击

罗伯特·蒙代尔,北京的荣誉市民,是科斯的仰慕者。听到老人家亲自策划一个关于中国经济改革的研讨会议,他建议要有一篇颂赞科斯的学术贡献的文章,而我是写这篇文章的适当人选。但科斯已经邀请我写这篇关于中国经改的开场主题,不是写科斯本人。我想,这里起笔说一下科斯的经济思想对中国的影响,也是适当的。这样做,我无可避免地要牵涉到自己，因为把科斯的思想介绍给中国同胞的只我一人。

一九七九我发表第一篇中语文章，题为《千规律，万规律，经济规律仅一条》。^{注三} 这个古怪的题目是回应早一年我读到的、中国著名经济学者孙冶方发表的《千规律，万规律，价值规律第一条》。^{注四} "文革"期间，孙先生说了这句话，被困坐牢七年。我当然同情他，但不同意他高举的马克思的价值与价格概念。我的长文只申述一点：资源稀缺，竞争无可避免；决定胜负要有准则，在无数可以采用的准则中，只有市价不会导致租值消散。^{注五} 我列举了多个不同的准则，包括排队轮

注三　张五常，《千规律，万规律，经济规律仅一条》，一九七九年十月《信报财经月刊》。

注四　孙冶方，《千规律，万规律，价值规律第一条》，一九七八年十月《光明日报》。

注五　租值消散是个重要论题，起于公共资源使用的分析：资源的租值，会因为没有约束的竞争使用，引起使用成本增加而消散了。由此引申，我指出只要不用市场价格，或市价被政策压着，其他的竞争准则一定会出现，而某程度上这些其他准则必会导致租值消散。从租值消散的角度来解释经济行为是一个重要的法门，可惜经济学行内不重视。我的经验是分析交易费用时，采用租值消散这个通道非常有效。

有关读物，见 Frank H. Knight, "Some Fallacies in the Interpretation of Social Cost," *Quarterly Journal of Economics*

购、论级分配等，指出必会有租值消散的浪费。只有市场价格这个准则没有，而市价的使用是基于有私产的存在。注六

很多年后我才知道该文在北京广泛流传，不少朋友说影响了后来中国差不多什么都收费的习惯。有系统地以中文解释科斯的界定资产权利与交易费用的理念，始于一九八二，见于《中国会走向资本主义的道路吗？》的中译。注七

一九八三年十一月，我开始热心地以中文下笔。《从科斯定律看共产政制》一九八四年一月发

(August 1924); H. Scott Gordon, "The Economic Theory of a Common Property Resource: The Fishery," *Journal of Political Economy* (April 1954); Steven N. S. Cheung, "The Structure of a Contract and the Theory of a Non-exclusive Resource," *Journal of Law and Economics* (April 1970); Idem, "A Theory of Price Control," *Journal of Law and Economics* (April 1974).

注六 采用市价是有费用的，但作为一个竞争准则，市价本身不会导致租值消散。关于采用市价的费用，见 R. H. Coase, "The Nature of the Firm," *Economica* (November 1937); George J. Stigler, "The Economics of Information," *Journal of Political Economy* (June 1961); Steven N. S. Cheung, "The Contractual Nature of the Firm," *Journal of Law and Economics* (April 1983).

注七 张五常，《中国会走向资本主义的道路吗？》，一九八二，重刊于张五常，《中国的前途》，一九八五年八月初版，再版多次，今天由香港花千树出版。

表。^{注八}该文详细地讨论了畜牧与种麦的例子。到今天，我发表了大约一千五百篇中语文章，一半是关于经济的。经济改革与政策分析约占总数的三分之一吧。我不是个改革者。然而，抗战期间在广西差不多饿死了，今天作为还活着的老人，我对国家的关心无从掩饰。外人是否同意无所谓，只要他们读我写出来的。我相信任何人读任何人的文章，多多少少会受到影响。

没有更好的时间，没有更好的地方，也许没有比我这个写手更好的推销员，在八十年代的中国推广科斯的思想。那时，国内的意识大门逐渐打开：同志们知道他们历来相信的不管用，要找新的去处。一九八二年五月，我获任香港大学的经济讲座教授，那是当时跟进中国发展的最佳位置。我对科斯的论著了然于胸，而众人皆知他是我的好朋友。^{注九}我是个中国文化与历史专家，同

注八　张五常，《从科斯定律看共产政制》，一九八四年一月二十七日发表于《信报》，转刊于《卖桔者言》，后者一九八四年十一月初版，再版无数次，今天由香港花千树出版。

注九　一九八〇年在底特律的美国经济学会的年会中，科斯催促我回到中国去，因为他听到中国有可能开放改革，而他认为我是向中国人解释经济制度运作的最佳人选。几个月后，我听到香港大学的经济讲座教授的位置将会空出。一九八二年五月获委此职，十八年后退休。

志们不能对我说我不懂中国——他们对外人例必这样说。我可以用中文动笔，没多久就写出读者认为通俗、风格鲜明的文字。这一切之上是科斯的原创思想，当时容易推销。如果当时的中国像今天这样，我是不会那么幸运的。

首先是交易费用的思维。中国人在早前的制度中非常熟识那无数的琐碎麻烦，例如要背诵口号，要排队轮购，要搞关系，要走后门。他们每天要花几个小时做这些事。当我说如果这些费用减低，收入会飙升，就是最顽固的旧制度维护者也难以应对。当时的交易费用奇高，怪事天天有，这些大家都清楚，但我需要时间与多篇文章才能说服中国的朋友，如果制度不改，交易费用不会下降。这方面，应归功于我。

要改为哪种制度呢？不容易说服。我一九七九的文章指出的观点：市场价格是唯一不会导致租值消散的准则，那些惯于排队数小时的人不难明白。然而，当我指出市价只能用于私有产权的制度，同志们不易接受。私字当头，在中国的文化传统里没有半点值得尊敬的含意，而私有产权更是直接地违反了北京对社会主义或共产主义的执著。

在这重要关键上，科斯的资产权利需要清楚界定这个思想大显神功。作为当时的经济科学推销员，我知道同样的产品有了个新的包装。一九八八年的秋天我带弗里德曼夫妇会见当时的中共中央总书记时，赵先生急于向米尔顿解释资产权利界定的重要。这对话有存案，在好几个地方发表过。成功地推销科斯的经济观给总书记也应归功于我。今天，在百度，那普及的中文搜索引擎，"科斯定律"的几个译法出现过不止十万次。

　　同样重要的，是所有权与使用权的分离。我用上好些例子申述。当时的香港，土地是政府或皇家所有，一幅官地的私人业主只持有一纸长期的租用合约。当我在洛杉矶加大做学生时，借钱购买了一部细小的菲亚特牌汽车。我是注册车主，银行是法定车主，但这两权的分离对我使用该车是没有影响的。科斯对权利界定的分析，在那一九六〇的鸿文中用上的多个精彩的实例，我看不到所有权是否私有对资源的使用有何重要。[注十] 这话题的出现，是因为当时我的注意力集中在一九八三开

[注十] R. H. Coase, "The Problem of Social Cost," *Journal of Law and Economics* (October 1960). 在早一篇同样重要的文章里，科斯写道："人们看来不明白的，是联邦传播委员要分配的，或者要在市场出售的，是以一件仪器传达信号的使用权。这样看问题，我们无须想到频率或无线广播的所有权谁属那边去。" Coase, "The Federal Communications Commission," *Journal of Law and Economics* (October 1959), p. 33.

始盛行的承包责任合约。我看到在逻辑上推到尽，这合约是准许私人使用资产但没有私人所有权。承包合约是这篇文章的重心所在，我稍后再详论。

让我跳到二〇〇六年八月于北京。周其仁给我看两本我自己的书：《中国的前途》（一九八五）与《再论中国》（一九八六）。[注十一]二者皆在香港出版，但被影印复制，扉页盖上一个"内部阅读"的印章。这些书是北京同志的内部或"秘密"读物。我从来没有那样高兴见到自己的书给人盗版（据说每书复印二千册）。在这两本结集中，科斯的影响是清楚而又广泛的。

第三节：合约的一般概念[注十二]

阿尔钦提出：任何社会，只要有稀缺，必有竞

注十一　张五常，《中国的前途》与《再论中国》，二者皆再版多次，目前由花千树出版。

注十二　二〇〇二年七月三十一日，弗里德曼九十大寿那天，我写了《合约的一般理论》。（张五常，《制度的选择》，第五章，第一节。）二〇〇七年五月二十四日到八月九日，我发表了十一篇关于经济学的缺环的文章。（张五常，《经济学的缺环》与《从安排角度看经济缺环》，后者分十篇，《壹周刊》。）这系列是为准备写这篇献给科斯的长文而作的。我认为这里的第三节，与上述的合并起来，会有一个完整的合约一般理论。

争，而决定胜者与负者的规则可以阐释为产权制度。作为他的入室弟子，加上后来受到中国经改的启发，我尝试从一个修改了的角度看世界。我的看法，是资源使用的竞争一定要受到约束，人类才可以生存，因为没有约束的竞争必然带来的租值消散，会灭绝人类。这些约束可以有不同的形式，或不同的权利结构，界定着经济制度的本质。

约束竞争的权利结构可分四大类，而任何社会通常是四类并存的。第一类是以资产界定权利，也即是私有产权了。第二类是以等级界定权利，也就是昔日中国的干部同志按资历级别的排列。^{注十三}第三类约束竞争的法门是通过法例管制。最后，竞争也可以受风俗或宗教的约束。

因为约束竞争含意着互相同意的行为，或暗或

注十三　安排有所不同，等级排列也可以在一个资本主义经济中的机构见到。然而，在共产制度下的同志等级排列，在一些重点上与一家私营企业的排列不同，前者较为近于政府设立的机构，例如一间公立医院或一间公立大学。单从等级排列看，共产制度与私营企业的主要分别，是前者的市民或员工没有权不参与，而转换工作要得到政府的批准。自由选择工作会导致同志等级排列制度的瓦解。当一九八三年底见到自由转业在珠江三角洲开始出现时，我立刻为文说中国的经济改革不会走回头路。在北方，工作的自由选择要到一九九二才开始，在邓小平于该年春天南下之后。

明，或自愿或强迫，这就含意着合约的存在。不一定是在市场以市价交易的合约。一九八二我说过，一个国家的宪法是合约。[注十四]私有产权、等级排列、法例管制、风俗宗教，等等，以我之见，都是不同形式的合约安排。

这里介绍的合约的广泛概念是需要的。原则上，我们可以把为了约束竞争而界定权利视作一类合约，而把交换权利或市场合约视作另一类（虽然市价也是约束竞争的局限）。[注十五]困难是这两类合约好些时不容易分开，而在中国，这两类合约往往是织合为一的。我们稍后将会讨论这后者的有趣安排。

为了理解中国，我以合约的关系来看社会里的人际互动。一九七九在广州，见到不同职业的等级排列的细微划分使我震撼。某级别的同志可以分享一部汽车，或每隔一天可得鸡蛋一只，或有权到市场买鱼但不需要排队。这些现象有启发力。我最初

[注十四] Cheung, *Will China Go Capitalist?* (London 1982), Hobart Paper 84, Section II.

[注十五] 市价是约束竞争的局限。正如亚当·斯密在《国富论》中写道："给我那我需要的，你可以获得这你需要的……" (Cannan edition, p. 18). 一个市价存在。

的解释，是天生下来人是不平等的，如果在一个"无产"的社会中每个人平等地"无产"，人权一定要不平等才能找到社会的均衡。再过两年，我看到深入一点的真理：中国的等级排列其实是合约的约束，在资产本身没有权利界定的情况下，需要有这种排列界定来减低在竞争下的租值消散。

这里的重要含意，是中国的经济改革必须有一种转移，要从以等级界定权利的制度转到以资产界定权利的制度，或者说要从一种合约安排转到另一种合约安排来约束竞争。这一点，我认为是解释中国三十年来的发展的重心所在。没有经过流血的革命而做到这种合约转移，可以视为奇迹，而我将指出，成功的关键，是中国用上一种刚好坐在上述的两种合约之间的另一种合约。后者称为承包责任合约。真正的奇迹可不是他们做到这重要的合约转移，而是他们达到的一种前所未见的经济制度。

既然在讨论一般性的理论，我要指出约束资源使用的竞争是需要费用的。这些费用被称为交易费用，实在有点误导。多年以来，我强调不同种类的交易费用只能在边际上分开，而验证假说所需要的，是指出这些费用的边际转变。我也曾经强调，交易费用不需要用金钱来量度，需要的是在不同的可以观察到的情况下，我们有本事排列交易费用的高低。不容易，但可以做到，我曾经无数次以观察到的现象转变来衡量交易费用的转变，做出准确的推断或解释。你可以不同意我对优质座位票价为何偏低的解释，[注十六]但多年以来我对中国将会发生的事的推断，得分之高，不可能是看水晶球的成绩。

除了从边际转变的角度看，不同种类的交易费用无法分开，这逼使我为交易费用下一个广泛的定义：涵盖鲁滨孙一人世界中不存在的所有费用。这样看，交易费用是可以在一个完全没有交易的情况下出现的。我认为应该称为制度费用才对，即是只有社会才能出现的费用。我的论点是交易（或制度）费用的起因，主要是为约束使用资源的竞争，或者从上文提出的广义合约安排看，起于用合约来约束竞争的需要。结论是：只要竞争存在，交易或制度费用一定存在。换言之，说一个社会没有这些费用是矛盾的说法。

一九八二年，我指出如果交易或制度费用不存在，不会有市场。评论科斯定律时，我写道：

> 如果广义的交易费用真的是零，我们要接受

[注十六] Steven N. S. Cheung, "Why Are Better Seats 'Underpriced'?" *Economic Inquiry* (1997), pp. 512-522.

消费者的意欲会不费分毫地准确表达；拍卖官与监察者会免费搜集与整理讯息；工作的人与其他生产要素会得到免费的指引，去从事与消费者的意欲完全吻合的产出；每个消费者获得的产品与服务，跟他的意欲会是一致的。仲裁者会免费地决定一个工作者或消费者的总收入：把他的边际产值，加上社会其他所有资源的租值的一个分成，这分成是依照大家不费分毫地同意的任何一种准则而决定的。如此推理，科斯的效果可以没有市价而达致。注十七

市场的存在是因为交易或社会费用不是零而起，跟科斯的经典公司分析和我早年的合约选择分析是没有冲突的。注十八 **说市场的出现是为了减低交易费用是近于定义性的了。然而，要解释座位票价或自助餐的安排，我们只需指出某些交易费用或制度费用的边际转变，但解释一个复杂的制度，或制度的转变，困难得多。**

注十七　Cheung, *Will China Go Capitalist? op. cit.*, Section III.

注十八　Coase, "The Nature of the Firm," *op. cit.*; Cheung, "Transaction Costs, Risk Aversion, and the Choice of Contractual Arrangements," *Journal of Law and Economics* (April 1969), pp. 23-42.

脑子闭塞，我的困难持续了差不多二十年。我不知道哪种交易或制度费用应该加进去来解释私产及市场的存在。我的广泛定义显示着这些费用无处不在，再没有加进的空间。二〇〇一年的一个晚上，我看到曙光：我们不是要加，而是要减这些费用，才能得到解答。

我跟着想到一篇只两页纸的文章，A. Bottomley一九六三发表的。[注十九]作者的论点，是的黎波里的草原极宜种植杏仁树，但因为草原公有，于是用作畜牧。[注二十]有价值的资源毫无约束地让公众使用的现象曾否出现过，我历来怀疑，但假设真有其事，租值消散是效果。那么，的黎波里的草原公用畜牧，其交易或制度费用是些什么呢？答案是消散了的租值！在我一九七四发表的关于价格管制的文章里，我指出租值消散是一种交易费用。[注二十一]的黎波里的例子，同样的看法比较困难，

[注十九] Bottomley, "The Effects of Common Ownership of Land Upon Resource Allocation in Tripolitania," *Land Economics* (February 1963).

[注二十] 在 Cheung, "The Structure of a Contract......" *op. cit.*，我补充说："维护在公众土地的植树投资的成本高，因为植在地上的树是固定了的，但牲畜却可以在晚上驱赶回家。"

[注二十一] Cheung, "A Theory of Price Control," *op. cit.*

但在两方面土地的租值消散真的是交易或制度费用。一方面，租值消散不会在一人世界发生；另一方面，成本（这里指费用）是最高的代价——的黎波里的畜牧代价是种植杏仁树的土地租值。定义说，把草原转作种植杏仁树的用途的总交易或制度费用，一定不会低于租值的消散，否则这用途的转变会出现了。跟着的含意是，如果我们能认定这些费用在哪方面有了转变，制度的转变可以推断。这正是一九八一年我推断中国会走向市场经济的道路的方法。

上述的观察，明显地说，如果的黎波里的草原是私有而种植了杏仁树，有三个结果。其一，土地的租值会上升而交易或制度费用会下降——这下降是减下去，在我们的例子中是租值代替了交易费用。其二，交易或制度费用的性质或类别是改变了，虽然这些费用永远不会下降至零。其三，从我们的广泛概念看，以合约安排来约束竞争，一种合约是取代了另一种。以我之见，后者是制度转变的正确意义。

上述的分析或看法，就是研究新制度经济学的人也可能不熟识，但对理解中国三十年来的经济改革却至关重要。尤其是我在交易或社会费用与合约安排的知识的增长，主要是从中国的经验学习得来的成果。

很不幸,制度的转变或合约安排的转变,不一定是朝减低交易费用或增加租值的方向走。亚当·斯密认为土地使用安排的转变是朝改进效率那方向走,不一定对。[注二十二]灾难性的安排单是二十世纪就出现过多次了。有时我想,人类可能有一天会因为自己的选择而毁灭自己。在个人争取利益极大化的假设下,人类自取灭亡的理论难以构想,虽然我尝试过好几次。[注二十三]我的老师赫舒拉发曾经以《力量的暗面》(*The Dark Side of the Force*)作为他出版的一本书名,这本书可能解释博弈理论今天在行内的盛行。我不赞同这个取向,因为我相信经济解释首要的,是辨识可以观察到的局限变动。可幸的是,以中国的经济改革而言,"力量的暗面"还没有大行其道。不管将来如何,一个古老而伟大的文化终于从深邃的黑洞中走出来了。我说过,这篇文章要回答的问题是:中国究竟做对了些什么才出现了大家见到的壮观表演呢?

[注二十二] 见 Cheung, *The Theory of Share Tenancy* (Chicago: University of Chicago Press, 1969), pp. 32-34.

[注二十三] 张五常,《从全球暖化说人类灭亡》,二〇〇七年二月二十二日;《世界末日好文章》,二〇〇七年三月八日。二文皆于《壹周刊》发表。

第四节：承包责任合约的演进

让我再次强调：中国经济改革的重点，是要把等级界定权利转到以资产界定权利的制度去。这是说，约束竞争的方法要改变。从前文提出的广义的合约概念看，约束竞争的合约安排要改变。这些合约不一定是大家熟知的市场合约，但还是合约，因为规限着人与人之间在社会竞争，什么可以做，什么不可以做。

要怎样才能把等级界定权利的制度转到资产界定权利的制度去呢？意识形态与政治考虑不论，八十年代初期出现的一个大困难，是这个转移含意着收入的分配要重新洗牌，既得利益分子不会接受。我当时的希望，是制度开始变换时会立刻导致总收入的跳升，以致收入排列位置下降了的人的收入还可以有增长。这收入跳升真的出现了：一九八三年，中国南方有几个地区的增长率高达百分之五十以上。虽然如此，制度的变换还是惹来此前的得益分子的反对。一九八五年四月，我为文建议国家出钱把等级权利买断。[注二十四]这建议带点幻想而又明显地困难，出乎意料地得到北京的一些言论支

注二十四　张五常，《官商的天堂》，一九八五年四月十二日发表于《信报》，其后转刊于《中国的前途》。

另一种补偿的方法出现：贪污。一九八四中期，贪污开始盛行。起初我是欣慰的，因为贪污是替代了早些时的后门交易。[注二十五]这清楚地显示着等级排列的制度开始瓦解。但当北京于一九八五公布他们计划把产品分类管制，我立刻大声疾呼，说中国正在走上"印度之路"，指出如果贪污的权利被管制法例界定了，中国的改革会停顿下来。[注二十六]警告之下，北京的支持声浪变得强大了。产品分类管制是放弃了的。

我不同意一些人的看法，他们认为在管制法例下的贪污对经济发展有利。中国的经验不支持这观点。贪污与经济增长之间的反向关联，推翻了贪污对经济有贡献的说法。但是，如果一定要说一点贪污的好处，那就是用金钱补偿特权分子或减少他们对改革的抗拒。我也不同意中国今天的贪污无所不在的观点。仍然普及，但比起八十年代与九十年代

[注二十五] "后门交易"是指偏袒的买卖。这些交易不是贪污，而是基于不同的等级排列有不同的权利。没有犯法。见张五常，《贪污的后患》，一九八五年一月三十日发表于《信报》，其后转刊于《中国的前途》。

[注二十六] 见 Steven N. S. Cheung, "A Simplistic General Equilibrium Theory of Corruption," *Contemporary Economic Policy* (July 1996).

初期，贪污下降了不少。我认识不少干部对自己的工作引以为傲，足以推翻贪污无处不在的说法。自一九九三起肃贪的行动有看头，而我将指出，肃贪是得到地区之间的竞争协助的。我认为比起其他亚洲国家，中国目前的贪污水平是偏低的。

从一种以合约界定权利的制度转到另一种，过程的初期中国幸运地得到一张有市价的合约协助。称为承包责任合约，用于农地功效立见。一九八六我写道：

> 那所谓承包责任合约，从最简单因而最完善的形式看，等于国家通过土地租约授予私有产权。这租约的年期可长可短，原则上是可以永久的。国家没有放弃土地的所有权，但使用权与收入权则为承租人独有。转让或出售可用转租的形式处理。政府的几种征收可以组合起来作为一个固定的租金，而因为这租金交给政府，就变为物业税。如果这土地租约是永久的，西方法律称 fee simple，加上租约可以自由转让，则称 fee simple absolute，是私产的最完善形式！注二十七

注二十七　Steven N. S. Cheung, "China in Transition: Where Is She Heading Now?" *Contemporary Policy Issues* (October 1986).

承包责任合约的演进

追查承包合约的发展,我得到同事蔡俊华慷慨地提供他搜集了多年的详尽资料,让我于一九八四发表一篇关于农业承包的文章。[注二十八] 故事从一九五八开始,人民公社在整个国家推行了。广泛的饥荒出现,而这悲伤的回忆持续了二十年。为了减少饥寒交迫,人民公社引进了一连串的修改措施。首先是工分制;跟着是生产大队;跟着大队改为小队;到了一九七八,承包责任合约开始出现。"承包"在中文的意思,是"你担保完成由我指定的,你可以做你的事"。起初这承包合约只用于生产队,一九八一伸延到农户去,附带着指明的产出目标。到一九八三,合约的条件改为农户担保交出一个定额,余下来的归农户所有。开始时官方的征收有好几项而又复杂,随着时日的消磨逐步简化,到二〇〇五取消了农业税。有一段时期政府有权以管制的价格购买农产品,这价管在九十年代初期取消了。

承包合约在农业很成功是没有疑问的。不同地区的农地以各区的人口平均分配,主要以人头算,而农地使用的转让过了不久就通过转包的形式出现。但当承包合约引用到工业时,遇到不少困难。

注二十八　张五常,《从"大锅饭"到"大包干"》,一九八四年十一月十五日发表于《信报》,其后转刊于《中国的前途》。

工业的运作，机械资产会变旧，也可能被盗去，而法律上国家职工不可以解雇。为了考查这些困难的底因，深圳选出三个青年协助我。工业承包合约的真实样本，有求必送。他们带我到工厂视察。有这些方便，我获得的却甚少。发展转变得太快，合约的条款不断地更改，使我难以找出有一般性的结论。

在这个时刻，大约一九八五吧，我强烈地建议把使用权与所有权分离，希望这样国营的企业能比较容易地私有化。[注二十九]一九八六年，我被邀请到北京的首都钢铁厂去研讨他们的承包合约安排。在他们的宿舍住了几晚，讲了一次话。十六年后——二〇〇二年四月二十二日——我被邀请到中共中央党校讲话。该校的商学院院长到机场接我，途中说当我在首钢讲话时，他在座。他说事后每个听众都受到警告，说不要相信我建议的把所有权与使用权分离，和把界定了的使用权推到尽头。英雄所见略同——中国人这样说——过了不久，使用权与所有权的分离成为邓小平说的"中国特色的社会主义"的基础。

注二十九　详细的解释可见于张五常，《再论中国》，第二与第三部分，共有九篇文章从一九八六年五月到一九八七年三月发表。

驶往党校途中，院长对我说，一九八六年他不可能想象自己有一天可以拥有一部电脑，但现在是隔一年换一部新的。听到这些话，我感触无限。像我们这些上了年纪的人，知道没多久之前中国的情况，比起对过往知得不多的年轻人，这些年发生的事来得更属奇迹了。从机场到党校是颇长的路程，我意识到这位上了年纪的干部对中国的奇迹感到骄傲，而国家必定有很多像他那样的人，在重要关头站起来准备拼搏。

第五节：承包合约的扩张与县际竞争的兴起

承包合约用于农业是成功的，虽然要好些时日才简化为今天的可以转让的土地租约。在这过程中，执政者逐步减少了他们的操控，偏向于界定土地的使用权利。九十年代初期农产品的价格管制取消了，二〇〇五年取消了农业税，使农业的承包成为不需要付税的长期租约。形式上还是承包。就是今天，农地的买卖称作"转包"。

把承包合约引用到工业去有困难。八十年代中期我考查这项目时，主要的困难是工业的资产要折旧。维修保养与再投资的责任谁属，上头政府与下面国企之间常有争吵。我建议过些解决方案，包括发行可以转让的股票。^{注三十}九十年代后期，发行股票开始实施，但主要是有垄断保障而有利润的国企。至于那些要亏蚀的无数国企，它们的资产净值早就下降至零。事实上，九十年代，执政的人要把亏蚀的国企免费送出去也不容易。

不同的时期有不同的困难。九十年代初期起，亏蚀的国企的困难再不是资产贬值——它们没有什么还可以折旧的了——而是要吃饭的国家职工没有补偿不能解雇。二十一世纪开始，这些亏蚀的国企成功地近于全面私有化，主要的协助是地价上升了。这点我将会解释。

令人失望的工业承包的经验，到头来却提供了一个有巨大价值的主意。大约一九八四年，那所谓"层层承包"的合约安排在工业出现。并不新奇，外间的工业称作"次承"，或称"分包"。西方称 subcontracting，而众所周知，工业或建筑业的"subs"往往是好几层串联起来的。如果一定要在中国经济改革中选出一项关键的发展，我的选择是从八十年代后期开始，农业的承包与工业的层层承包组合在一起。是非常重要的成就：这组

注三十　见注二十九的文章，及张五常，《中国的经济革命》(1993)，二〇〇二年四月增订再版（花千树出版有限公司）。

合不是引用到个别农户或个别国企，而是引用到有地理界线划分的地区去。我认为这是今天中国的经济制度的重心所在。

一个长期不断地跟进这个制度的发展的人，可能觉得非常复杂，但到后来尘埃渐定，则可以看到这制度是直截了当而又理性的。没有在其他地方出现过。虽然制度中的每一部分都不是新的，但组合的方法与形式是创新而又有效能。

承包合约的组合引用到地区去的初期，不同地区的安排往往不同，变动频繁，要到大约一九九四这制度整体的共同特征才可以辨识。我开始领略到这制度有超凡之处，是一九九七我到昆山考查那里的发展。地区之间的激烈竞争是我前所未见的。二〇〇〇年通缩终结，地区竞争的惊人活力使我震撼，但我要到二〇〇四的年底才能解通这制度运作的密码。虽然在不同的程度上，地区之间的竞争其他国家都有，但我将申述，从性质与活力这两方面看，中国的地区竞争自成一家，天下独有。

不怀疑执掌政权的人有本领，但我认为今天的中国制度不是个别天才想出来的。这制度是被经济的压力逼出来——有那么多人要吃饭，改革的浪潮震耳欲聋。处理当时的风起水涌，指导的原则可不是邓小平说过的名句:"摸着石头过河",而是寡言的邓老曾经说的:"试一试,看一看。"

在细说这地区竞争制度之前,我要澄清一些名词。每个地区当然有它的专有名词,但它们的普通名词——市、镇等——可以有混淆。有些普通名词不同是因为起名于不同的时间,也有些经特别处理,直接由北京管辖。我喜欢用自己的地区分类,是干部朋友之间一致认同的。

中国的地区从上而下分七层,每层由地理界线划分,下一层必在上一层之内。最高层是国家,跟着到省,到市,到县,到镇,到村,最后到户。这七层是从上而下地以承包合约串联起来的。上下连串,但左右不连。地区竞争于是在有同样承包责任的地区出现,即是同层的不同地区互相竞争。

经济权力愈大,地区竞争愈激烈。今天的中国,主要的经济权力不在村,不在镇,不在市,不在省,也不在北京,而是在县的手上。理由是:决定使用土地的权力落在县之手。中央与次一层的省政府提供关于土地及其他经济政策的指导,有权更改地区的划分界线,有权调动地区的干部或把他们革职,也可以把不同地区的税收再分配。

一个发展中的国家,决定土地使用的权力最重要。没有土地就没有什么可以发展。土地得到有效率的运用，其他皆次要。如果在竞争下土地的租值上升，经济是在增长。科技的改进与资产及知识的积累当然重要——目前中国正迈步向这些方面走：私营的科技研究投资的增长率，今天的中国冠于地球。然而，如果人民吃不饱，科技及投资是没有什么用场的。处理好土地的使用，让广大的群众脱离饥寒交迫之境，经济会因为有储蓄、投资与科技改进的支持而上升。

竞争的激烈程度决定着土地使用效率的高低。人与人之间竞争，户与户之间竞争，机构与机构之间竞争——传统的经济分析，这些是所有的竞争了。中国的情况，是在同层的地区互相竞争，而因为县的经济权力最大，这层的竞争最激烈。以我之见，多加了一层竞争是回答我说的"中国问题"的重要新意。

"县"往往被翻译为"郡"（county）。这是不对的。在中国，"市"的面积很大。平均一个市有八点六个县。二〇〇六年底，官方的统计，是整个国家有二千八百六十个县（或是同等级别的地区），各有高度的关于土地使用及日常经济决策的自主权。县的平均面积约三千平方公里，但差异很大。人口稀少的西部，县的面积一般是庞大的。人烟稠

密的东部，县的面积约一千平方公里。我估计县的平均人口约四十五万，差异也是大的。注三十一

问题仍在——中心问题仍在：为什么县与县之间的竞争会是那样激烈呢？其他国家不是也有不同层面的地区划分吗？在中国经济制度的合约结构中，究竟是哪些基本因素促成地区之间的激烈竞争的局面，从而出现了大家都见到的近于奇观的经济增长？

第六节：县制度的佃农分成

中国的经济改革可分阶段看。第一阶段大约从一九八〇到邓小平退休的一九九二。这阶段的发展，主要是从以前的等级排列权利转到以资产界定权利那边去，以一九八七年十二月一日深圳拍卖土地（国家首次）为高峰。这拍卖是出售长期的土地使用合约，没有私人所有权。该市的干部说是依照我的建议：早些时，我对他们解释，

注三十一　通过承包合约而把经济权力授予县，这几年出现了一个有趣的议论：中国应该取消城市吗？赞成的认为：经济权力落在县之手，但政权却是城市的干部较高，冲突不容易避免，这会扰乱整个制度的运作。是复杂的话题，我没有跟进。二〇〇七财政年度起，县直接汇报财务事项到省政府，跳过了市，但其他政权还是市高于县。

出售土地差不多是唯一能让他们获取足够资金来发展该市的办法，而他们要让私营的发展商人表演专业的运作。注三十二

在这阶段，经济发展集中在中国南部的珠江三角洲。开放改革之前，这地区相对上遭到漠视或贬低，庞大的国营企业或政府保护的垄断机构寥寥无几。香港的商人或投资者身先士卒，带进资金、科技与管理知识。相比之下，当时的长江三角洲，有权有势的国企抗拒竞争，与南部只需几天甚至几个小时可以获得私营的商业牌照相比，是两回事。

在长三角，市场的冲击大约始于一九九三。神奇地，只八九年，差不多所有重要的经济数字，长三角超越了珠三角。这是中国改革的第二阶段，由朱镕基掌管经济。从一九九三至二〇〇〇这七个年头，是中国的困难时刻：开始时通胀如脱缰之马，贪污广泛，人民币崩溃，跟着是严厉控制借贷与消费，重击贪污，再跟着是通缩与房地产市场兵败山倒。然而，就是在这些困扰的情况下，长三角出现了爆炸性的发展，其效应伸延到内陆的中、西部去。我们或可举出好些理由来解释这奇迹的出现，

注三十二　一九八六年六月，我发表了一篇分析卖地有三个好处的文章。深圳的干部喜欢该文，一九八七年的春天请我去商讨。张五常，《出售土地一举三得》，一九八六年六月二十五日于《信报》发表，其后转刊于《再论中国》。

但我认为主要的原因,是县的竞争制度刚好在那时形成,开始发挥效应了。

在情在理,在上述的恶劣经济环境下,长三角要超越起步早十年的珠三角是不可能的,但却发生了。^{注三十三}**我的解释,是那一九九四形成的县制度在长三角运作得较好。在南方,私营的企业已经在**

注三十三　一九八八年的秋天,我带弗里德曼夫妇游览长三角一带。米尔顿见到小贩在烂泥路上经营是高兴的,后来在北京会见总书记时,他对总书记说街头小贩要贿赂才能拿得牌照。苏州的干部带我们去参观那里的乡镇企业,是令人尴尬的。晚宴上,苏州的一位副市长与米尔顿争论国营企业的优越性。一九九三年的秋天,我再带弗里德曼夫妇到中国。上海的一条大街灯火通明,当我们的旅游大车经过随行朋友的商店时,大家一起鼓掌。弗氏夫妇一九九八再到上海半天,米尔顿不相信自己见到的。

弗氏夫妇的中国行有两个插曲这里要存案。其一是我给米尔顿上了一课中国经济学。一九八八在上海,在街上走,肚子饿,见到街上一个小贩卖饺子。我拿出钱包,但发觉单是钱不管用,还要粮票。一个过路的人见我跟小贩争议,送给我一小叠粮票。我大喜,米尔顿问我为何那么高兴,我说:"那位先生免费地给我这些粮票。你可以想象粮票一文不值吗?这个城市将要爆炸!"果然爆炸。第二个插曲是米尔顿输了一次辩论!一九九三年在成都,四川的省长接见我们。米尔顿教该省长怎样改革才对,说要斩掉老鼠的尾巴,不要一寸一寸地斩,为了减少痛苦,要一次过地把整条尾巴斩掉。省长回应:"教授呀,我们这只老鼠有那么多条尾巴,不知要先斩哪条才对。"米尔顿不能回应。伤感的是,那位省长今天不在了。是个勇敢的人,以大胆批评知名,听说后来他得不到北京的支持了。

早前的合约安排下落地生根。工厂到处乱放,既不整齐也不清洁,但投资者是下了注的。换言之,南方缺少了土地使用的调整弹性,减少了县与县之间的竞争效能。不是说南方的县不竞争,而是他们没有北方那种调整土地使用的大弹性。这经验也教训我们,不用政府策划而单靠市场必然较有效率的看法是错的。世界级的工业园在长三角一带冒起,美观的园艺与现代化的设施,是例行地由县的干部策划。他们是为市场策划的!他们知道好东西会卖得较好。他们也知道,如果策划的卖不出去,可能被革职。

在县与上头之间有一条分配收入的方程式,对鼓励竞争重要。简略地说,发展初期,是下面承包的把一个固定的款额交给上头。往往引起争吵,因为发展得好而要交得多的地区认为是被剥削了。分成的安排于是引进,争吵又出现,因为不同的地区要上缴的分成率不同。

这就带来一九九四的一项重要发展。从那时到今天,一个地区或县的工业投资者要付百分之十七的产品增值税,而这个税率是全国一致的。县本身的分成,是此税的四分之一,也即是产品增值的百分之四点二五。另一方面,一间小企业可以选择支付百分之四至六的商业税(视乎企业的性质而定）来代替。利润或所得税是有钱赚才交，这里我们不管。我们的讨论也可以不管商业税——没有利润也要付的。增值税给政府带来最高的收入，县干部最关心此税。我们的分析集中在增值税：产出价值扣除原料与其他一些琐碎费用之后的百分之十七。

问题是增值的百分之十七的抽取究竟是税，还是租呢？我认为是租而不是税。有两个理由。其一是任何投资者，只要用土地或房产从事生产的，都要付此税。其二是只要有产出，不管有没有利润，都要付此税。

一九八六我写道：

> 在古时的中国，正如中世纪的欧洲，"租"与"税"的意思是相同的。当一个收租的封建地主负上一个"政府"的责任主持正义与提供保护时，收租就称为抽税。注三十四

争论是租还是税有点无聊，问题是在经济学的传统中，说争取最高的税收必遭批评，但说争取最高的租金收入则往往被认可。真理是，有经济效率的土地使用，租金一定要算，不管是由地主还是

注三十四　Cheung, "China in Transition......," *op. cit*.

由政府收取。收得的租金要怎样花是另一回事。我的论点,是如果土地全部使用,在县与县之间的竞争下,争取最高的总租值是与高效率一致的。这不是说投资者会因而无利可图。他们预期的收入,除去要上缴的租(税)之外,要足以弥补利息成本,而如果因为他们的投资而经济增长了,他们的收入可以高于预期。事实上,大部分的投资者在县的制度下收获甚佳,尤其是二〇〇〇年之后。这是说,经济增长带来的土地租值上升,含意着的收入增加会落在投资者、劳工与农民的手上。纵观二〇〇三开始的农产品的相对价格上升,上述的收入增加很有看头。

全国一致的百分之十七的增值税是多番与不同的地区商讨后才达到的。明显是分成租金,所以明显的是佃农分成制,一方面是投资者与县政府分成,另一方面是县与上头高层分成。这里有一个分析难题困扰了我好几个月。四十年前我发表《佃农理论》,其中偏离传统的一个要点,是我让分成的百分比变动来推出有效率的结论。亚洲的农业资料明确地显示,佃农分成的比率会因为土地的质量与地点不同而有相当大的变化。然而,这里提到的增值税,是分成租金,却是全国用上同一的税率。怎可以有经济效率呢?如果没有,中国的经济怎可以在这分成安排下加速增长?

一天晚上我突然想起做研究生时读到的一个马歇尔的注脚,立刻从床上跳起来去找它。马歇尔认为与固定租金相比,分成租金无效率。但他补加了一个注脚:

> 如果佃农分成的地主能自由地为自己的利益调整资本,并且与佃农协商,指明农作劳力的投入量,几何上可以证明,地主会这样调整来强迫农户的耕耘密度与在英国的固定租金制度一样,而地主的分成收入,会与固定租金相等。注三十五

这注脚我当年做出如下的回应:

> 马歇尔没有提供几何证明,如果试证,他会否更改这个注脚是有趣的猜测。这猜测有趣是因为他想象的效果,在一些特殊的情况下是对的,但一般而言却是错了。错了,因为马歇尔不让分成的百分率变动。注三十六

基于马歇尔的注脚与我的回应,假设县政府是地主,我问县的资本投入,要多少才能担保一个不

注三十五　Alfred Marshall, *Principles of Economics* (8th ed., 1920: London; Macmillan Co. 1956), p. 536, note 2.

注三十六　Cheung, *The Theory of Share Tenancy, op. cit.*, p. 45.

变的分成率会一般地达到有经济效率的情况。二〇〇四年底我找到的答案，是县向"佃农"分成的投资者收取的地价，可以是负值！把土地视作地主提供的资本，可以用负地价代表地主提供着无限的调整机能，只要分成的百分率落在一个不离谱的范围，在这机能下有效率所需的边际价值相等的条件永远可以达到。

说负地价，我的意思是当一个投资者到一个县考虑投资产出，县政府不仅可以免费提供改进了的土地，也可能免费为投资者建造厂房，或把若干年从投资者交出的增值税中的县的分成的一部分，送给投资者。当然，不是所有的县都值得投资，例如设厂于荒山野岭没有意思。社会利益不论，负地价可以去到的尽头，是县的税收足以填补收回农地与改进为工商业用途的成本利息。这方面，下一节会再分析。

二〇〇六年北京开始禁止某些县用负地价，显示着他们不明白县的佃农分成制度的运作。也可能不是不明白。一个困难是中国的人口分布可能过于集中在热门地带，而较为长远的发展，略为平均的人口分布可能较上算。这话题我写过，但没有提出解决的方案。正如科斯和我在分析公司的本质时提及，有些事情是没有市场价格指引的，错误的决策往往只能事后才知道。

第七节：分成方程式的效果

二〇〇五年的一个晚上，一个遥远的县的县长给我电话，说他碰巧到了我家邻近，要来倾谈一下。进门后，他脱掉鞋子，躺在沙发上好一阵，然后问："教授呀，可否给我一杯葡萄酒？"当然可以。

我知道发生了什么事。这样的县干部，全国东奔西跑寻求投资者。当一个招商集会在某城市举行，消息传出，无数的县干部会闻风而至。这些日子一个县干部一个晚上吃几顿晚餐是寻常事。

一个三十万人口的县往往有五百个招商员。二〇〇五年，安徽某县举办选美比赛，要选出美丽、迷人而又懂得说话的女士做招商队长。舆论破口大骂，县长回应："美丽是资产，不利用可惜。"

需要一个商业牌照吗？县政府会派人代你奔走。要建筑许可证吗？他们给你担保。不喜欢那不洁的小溪流过你的场地吗？他们可能给你建造一个小湖。他们帮你找设计师，找建筑商，而准备投产时，会协助你聘请员工，收的费用合理。是的，县有招工队，替投资者招工。他们会向你推销他们的廉价电力，推销他们的公园与娱乐，推销他们的方便交通，水电供应，光辉历史，甚至他们的女孩有多漂亮——我没有夸张！

中国地区之间的激烈竞争，外间没有见过。为什么呢？一个因素是分成的方程式。这里谈此式，其他过后才说。

说过了，投资者要付百分之十七的产品增值税。县取此税的四分之一，即产品增值的百分之四点二五。土地出售的收入，如果是正数，县收百分之七十五，百分之二十五交上头。这百分率不是一致的：地点较佳的县，分账率会较低。我遇到过的县干部，没有谁管上头层面怎样分他们交上去的。

土地的成本不低。有两部分。第一部分是农民交出农地要受到补偿。用百分之五的折现率，我估计二○○六年这补偿是三至五倍农地租值的折现。县政府与农民的争吵有所闻，但不是媒体报道那样普遍。有时县干部从中骗取些私下钱，而缺乏资金的县可能欠农民一段长时日。

把农地改进做工商业用地的开发成本更高。二○○六年，这成本约六万元人民币一亩（六百六十平方米），大约比补偿农民高一倍。这些改进包括建造马路、引进电、水、煤气、排污、电话电视与电脑的线路、路灯、园艺等。这些改进是土地出售之前做好的。今天,就是档次较低的新工业用地,比我熟识的在美国华盛顿州的好。最高档次的,例如苏州工业园,是我见过的最好的了。中国的农民是超凡的种植能手——他们往往搬动移植五十年以上的树——而你无法斗得过 Arthur Lewis 说的"无限"人手供应:园艺工人每一长天的工资五美元。注三十七

二〇〇六年我作过估计,用一个发展略有看头的县的资料,得到如下的结果。假设一块工业用地建上容积率零点八的厂房,投产时用上最常见的劳工密度,县政府每年拿得的产品增值的百分之四点二五大约是工业用地的总成本的百分之十二。

注三十七 这是二〇〇四年的数字,在中国历史上农民的收入增长得最快的时刻。是日工的工资,二〇〇七年升至八点五美元左右。这个数字在不同的地区有别,是我到中国农村摄影时的大约平均估计。从二〇〇三到二〇〇五年,我摄得的作品让我出版了七本摄影集。因此,虽然我对中国农民生活的衡量与他家的报告相差很远,其实是基于漫长而又集中的实地调查所得,方法跟一九七二我在华盛顿州调查苹果与蜜蜂时用上的一样。见 Steven N. S. Cheung, "The Fable of the Bees: An Economic Investigation," *Journal of Law and Economics* (April 1973), pp. 11-33.

不包括行政费用，但可见一个县可以把工业用地送出，再补贴投资者一小点，还不用亏蚀。

毫无疑问，在同一县内，同样的工业用地同期出售，地价可以很不相同。除了久不久引起非议的偏袒成交，地价不同不代表价格分歧。县的干部要选择投资者。他们要争取的不单是增值税，还要顾及的是投资者带来的声望，要顾及行业是否与县里的其他行业合得来。不难见到，当一个投资者的项目可以引进很多其他好处时，县政府卖地的负地价可以跌到增值税的收入低于填补土地成本的利息。

县的干部可能贪污，但多年来我没有遇到一个愚蠢的。他们知道土地与土地之间的边际社会收益要相等才能为县及为自己取得最高的收入，如果同样的土地售价相同，他们的目的不可能达到。他们也知道准确的判断非常困难，所以常派调查员到有成就的县去考察。跟县干部的多次倾谈中，他们的常识与他们永远关注着互补性、招徕力、交通水电、娱乐等事项的意识，令我印象难忘。我不是说县干部从来不贪污，但我没有遇到过一个投资者不认为自己有特别的关系可以利用。是的，说服每个投资的他或她有特殊关系，县干部的本领绝对是世界级！

让我再说，虽然增值税率与此税的摊分率是全国一致的，其他的分账率并不一致。土地出售所得的分账率不一。不热门的县，此率要高一点才能填补土地的成本。方程式中的分账奖金也要一提。如果投资者是来自国外的，以他把钱放进指定的银行算，我知道一个县的干部会分得百分之一点五到百分之二。来自国内，奖金是投资的百分之一。这些其实是佣金，由县干部分享。早期条件欠佳的县的奖金高达投资额的百分之五。发展有成逐步减少。有一个热门地区，奖金是投资额的百分之零点零五。这个奖金分账率可以商议，正如房地产交易的佣金在中国可以商议。我倾谈过的县干部多数认为，奖金率足以鼓励他们东奔西跑。

第八节：县现象的经济解释

县与县之间的激烈竞争不寻常。我认为那是中国在困难的九十年代还有急速发展的主要原因。大约二〇〇四年越南把这中国制度抄过去——有人说是得到我的文章的提点——那里的经济也起飞了。这制度不难抄袭，但需要地区没有顽固的利益阶层，也要有像中国共产党那样的组织来推行。像朝鲜与古巴那样的国家，要尝试成功机会很不错。

不难抄袭，但解释却非常困难。不容易明白为什么这制度运作得那么好。我只一个晚上就打开了佃农分成之谜，却要三年的长日子才能解通中国的密码。困难所在，是我们面对的是个复杂的合约制度，此前没有见过。演变迅速，过程中不同的地区有不同的安排，要到尘埃渐定才依稀地见到一个可以理解的图案。要长时日才能看到关键的要素，而当我认为找到了这些，另一些重要的碎片还是缺少了。跟进中国的经济改革学得很多，使我对合约与交易或制度费用的理解提升到一个新层面，让我能用有一般性的理论去找寻那些缺少了的，然后把碎片组合，砌成一幅看得明白的图画。

让我从一九六九的春天说起吧。当时科斯和我到温哥华参加一个渔业研讨会议。在座有人提出，因为公海的鱼一般游很远，渔业私产化公海要独占，所以要有垄断权；这样，市场的鱼价会是垄断之价。我立刻回应："如果地球上所有的农地都是我的，我一定要分租给无数的农户耕耘；农户之间会竞争，所以农产品之价必定是竞争市场的价格。"

名义上，今天北京是地球上最大的地主，拥有中国天下全部土地的所有权。他们把土地以五十年长约租出，二〇〇七年公布租约期满后自动续约，指明政府有特别需要时可支付补偿来收回土地。他们接受了使用权要清楚地界定为私有，也知道要广泛地这样做，于是把有了界定的使用权下放，达到每户每家。为了维护有秩序的权利下放，他们知道承包合约可行，在经济压力下层层承包的合约安排就出现了。今天一个局外人拿着不同地区层面的文件研究内里的法规条文，很难看得出字里行间含意着的是一连串的承包合约。这些文件其实是早前的承包合约经过了修改而演变出来的。

不同的地区层面是垂直或上下串联，同层或左右不连。这是同层的地区互相竞争的一个主要原因，而由于县的经济权力最大，这一层的竞争最激烈。火上加油，权利的界定的原则无处不用。县的地理界线划分当然清楚，而县干部的权力与责任的划分来得那么清晰，今天的县无疑是一级的商业机构了。性质类同的商业机构互相竞争，是县与县之间的激烈竞争的另一个理由。

再火上加油，县干部的奖赏按成绩算。政治游戏与贪污无疑存在，但这些行为，就是先进之邦的市场经济中的大商业机构也有。除了前文提到的奖赏方程式，县干部的应酬费用相当慷慨，视乎那个县能赚多少钱。每个干部可以按建筑成本作价购买一间住所，而工作成绩好有机会升职。有一个流行的"五十六岁的假说"：六十退休，到了五十六而积蓄不够，干部贪污的倾向上升。他们也告诉我，能干的县干部不难有外间的商业机构招手，因为管理一个县其实是管理一盘生意。

一九九四全面引进的产品增值税，又再火上加油。那是佃农分成。我早期的论著指出，在佃农制度下，地主关心农户的操作履行比固定租金为甚，因为地主的收入如何要看佃农的工作表现。注三十八一个鲜明的例子可以示范县与县之间的热烈竞争。那是购物商场。一个县可以视作一个庞大的购物商场，由一家企业管理。租用这商场的客户可比作县的投资者。商场租客交一个固定的最低租金（等于投资者付一个固定的地价），加一个分成租金（等于政府收的增值税），而我们知道因为有分成，商场的大业主会小心地选择租客，多方面给租客提供服务。也正如商场给予有号召力的客户不少优惠条件，县对有号召力的投资者也提供不少优惠

注三十八　Cheung, *The Theory of Share Tenancy, op. cit.*, pp. 72-79.

了。如果整个国家满是这样的购物商场,做类同的生意但每个商场是独立经营的,他们竞争的激烈可以断言。

比起上述假设的购物商场,县的制度对鼓励竞争犹有过之。这是因为县要对上层作交代或报告。上层不仅鼓励竞争——他们强迫这竞争的出现。说到底,百分之七十五的增值税是上层收的。这是层层承包促长竞争的激烈性的原因。

让我们回到承包责任这个制度去深入一点地理解县与县之间的竞争。这个制度演进时,使用权的界定——因而有私产——是织进了市场合约中。从科斯的定律看,市场的运作分两步。第一步是界定私有产权,我的看法是以合约来约束资源使用的竞争。第二步是市场本身的出现,通过有市价的合约来交换资源的使用或产品的权利。

承包责任制是另一种安排。使用权的界定与市场成交是结合在同一合约中。一个投资于县的人,通常只签一份几页纸的合约,里面说明土地面积、地点与地价,他的权利和义务,以及双方履行责任的期限。地产证或地契要等投资者的钱汇到指定的银行几个月后才拿得。签好了的合约可以转让,但如果投资者要到银行借钱,有地契在手就比较方便了。

问题是为什么跟科斯的分两步处理相比,把产权织进了市场合约会增加竞争的效应呢?答案是在织合的安排下,投资者要履行责任。付钱之外,投资者要在合约指定的期间履行指定的项目才能获取土地的使用权。这是说,付价之外,承包合约是授予值得的优胜者。错误的判断当然可能,而取巧的投资者不罕有,例如只建造围墙而不再建什么。地价下跌之际县干部可能忙顾左右,但当经济转热他们会收回不履行合约的土地。当大跌了的地价在二〇〇〇年掉头上升时,不少投资者哭出声来,但履行合约的却在偷笑。

上述的织合安排不是中国独有的。正如科斯指出,好些国家的租约或雇用合约往往有类似的安排,而我在上文指出了购物商场的合约安排很类似。我也曾指出,中国的县制度的每一部分都不是新的。新而重要的是这些部分的组合,通过承包责任合约的扩张:使用权的授予是换取履行,而这基本原则到处用。尤其是,在工业发展中,政府机构与私人企业之间的合约安排,通过上述的织合、佃农分成与层层承包的串联,是令人敬畏的经济力量带来的效果,在一个有超过十亿贫困人口的时代,领导者既有勇气也有智慧去执行"试一试,看一看"这个原则。

通过串联承包合约而形成的权利结构，使我联想到一个国家的宪法，但在中国，这合约结构中的条件可以商讨，所以安排的弹性比较高，而一般来说，中国的安排的市场倾向，远比我知道的其他国家的宪法明显。二〇〇四年二月，我发表了《还不是修宪的时候》那篇长文，试图阻止当时正在进行的修宪工作。注三十九当时我指出，中国的经济制度既特别而又重要，北京要先研究这制度的性质，指出重要的环节，然后写进宪法去。北京没有接受我的建议，而他们跟着修改了的宪法，与他们的经济制度的结构是扯不上关系的。北京显然没有充分地赏识他们自己做得对，做得漂亮，做得精彩。

从研究中国的经验中我们得到四个重要的含意。第一，私产与市场对改进人民的生活无疑重要，但我们一定要加进界定经济制度的合约结构与安排来看问题。这篇文章示范着的，是中国的经济制度牵涉着一个广泛而又复杂的合约结构，相近的没有出现过。这种安排促成的县际竞争，对我来说，关键地解释了"中国的问题"。当然，从科

注三十九　张五常，《还不是修宪的时候》，二〇〇四年二月十六日，《信报》。

学的角度衡量，我们不能排除还有其他更有效率的合约安排，只是人类没有尝试过。从这个世纪转换的时候看，以一个天然资源相对地贫乏的国家而言，我认为中国的经济制度是人类历史上对经济增长最有效的制度。

第二，人民与社会面对的局限条件如何，对界定经济制度的合约结构的选择有决定性。以县为基础的制度在中国运作得好。那是个人口众多而天然资源稀少的国家，上苍赐予的只是一个聪明而又能刻苦耐劳的民族。换作一个天然资源丰富的国家，采用中国的经济制度不一定有好效果。

第三，经济增长的速度与界定经济制度的合约结构是息息相关的。我曾提及，县干部给同意赶工的投资者优先考虑，对赶工例行地帮忙。分账的方程式指明，县干部的收入是直接及正数地跟增长的速度联系着的。这样看，北京的调控政策频频出错：当他们见到增长年率高于百分之八或九时，远高于外国的，就认为经济"过热"，要用宏观调控来冷却经济。近距离地观察了中国三十年，我认为那里的经济波动主要来自政策的转变，而西方经常提及的内部性的"商业周期"，中国一丝也看不到。

最后，我认为如果没有政府或共产党的主持，中国的经济制度不会近于奇迹地发展起来。然而，在本文不愉快的后记中我指出，这近于奇迹的发展只持续了二十九年。是成是败，政府的存在对中国经济制度的发展是重要的。近几年在中国推出的愚蠢政策，一般来自从西方回归的经济学博士的凭空想象。这是经济学的悲哀。

第九节：县际竞争的其他效应

这些日子，读中国媒体报道的经济政策要小心。撰稿的人不是说谎，但往往误导，因为他们一般不理解中国的经济制度。县有相当大的经济决策自主权，好些时没有执行北京公布的政策。最低工资的引进，不同的县有很大的时间差别，而一些县只说他们有最低工资但不强迫。当北京宣称百分之七十的新建公寓单位要约束在九十平方米以下，一些地区公布有一两个这样的项目，其他地区则置之不理。报章的头条说一个外来的人不能购买超过一个住宅单位，深圳目前执行，上海说没有听过。注四十

注四十　二〇〇七年十一月，上海也引进这规定，但该市的不同地区各自有法避去。可以说，上海没有真的执行这个规定。深圳起初是严厉执行的，过了不久可以用大约四千美元购买另一条通道，后来楼价大跌，政府忙顾左右。

这不是说北京失控。他们是控制着的，但地区干部知道哪些真的要执行，哪些只是投石问路。他们懂得衡量上头传达下来的文件有多认真。北京征求地区的意见常有，而推了出来的政策可能悄悄地取消但没有公布。有些村落有民主投票，有些没有，而有投票的引进的时间很不相同。

我认为上述的混乱画面可不是真的混乱，而是起自地区的自主权与他们之间对政策的取向有别。一个县是否把一项政策用作粉饰橱窗，考虑的是这政策会否有助他们的竞争。为了增加县的产品增值税收，为了生存，县的干部要引进投资者，他们知道劣政策会把投资者赶走。如果北京坚持要执行一项政策，县会接受，但如果这政策有损地区的利益，他们会投诉。投诉够多往往有效。

发展到今天，县制度的权力结构是不容易拆除的了——这是支持着可以乐观地认为快速的经济增长还可持续一段长时日的主要原因。困难在于地区无权过问的事项：货币制度，外汇管制，对外政策，言论与宗教自由，国家操控的教育与医疗，传媒通讯，以及庞大的有垄断性的国企。

我担心北京对这个经济制度的运作理解不足，因为有迹象显示，他们正在尝试改动这个制度。^{注四十一}我认为只要把这制度精细地调校一下，就会变得坚固了。正如我在二〇〇四年二月的长文指出，层层承包以分成合约串联，在最理想的安排下，任何一个单位或成员的界定权利受到侵犯，某程度整个连串的所有成员都要付出这侵犯的代价。

因为地区或县的竞争，中外合资的合约发展成为一种特别的专利使用合约，每项的使用费可以不受管制地汇到外国的银行。我曾经研究过发明专利的使用合约好几年，知道监管这些合约的履行很困难，但以合资合约从事，有外来的作为董事在场监察，收钱就容易得多了。这是外资蜂拥到中国来的其中一个原因。周燕奇迹地拿得一批合资合约的真版本，赢得一篇不错的博士论文。我邀请了她为这个会议写一篇摘要，这里不多说。

因为县的竞争，工业类聚的集中发展非常显

注四十一　二〇〇七年一月一日，北京给县增加了两项规定。其一是显著地提升了收回农地时给农民的补偿。这是判断性的。其二是出售任何用作建筑的土地，要通过拍卖。原则上，这后者对县制度的运作不利，但有躲避之方。县会把土地的投资项目写得特别，广告若隐若现，通告时间缩短。这样，洽商好了的投资者通常是拍卖的胜出者。

著。中国的产品今天泛滥地球，但外间的人很少知道工业的地区集中与专业的程度。佛山的陶瓷产出历来有名，我邀请了李俊慧为工业类聚提供一文，因为她在佛山大学任职。

因为县的竞争，国营企业的私有化受到压力要加速。世纪转换，地价的上升大大地协助了这私有化的进程。较高的地价让地区政府有钱补偿解散国家职工，拿开了最大的障碍。国企的买家会把原先位于市区的物业出售，搬到地价较低的工业区去。长沙的国企私有化的速度可能破了世界纪录。我安排了那里的副市长刘晓明写有关文章，因为是他主导这发展的。

县的竞争也协助了减少贪污。有同样条件的地区，只有无知的投资者会到一个贪污知名的县下注。有经验的投资者知道贿赂是一项成本，早期在中国南方的厂家例行地把这些成本算进产品售价之内。不是所有贪污都消失了，而是与九十年代初期相比，减少了很多。跟我谈过的干部都同意县与县之间的竞争有助减少贪污。

最后，我认为过去十至十五年的合约选择的高度自由——除了上文提到的地区承包合约的串联——也是县际竞争的效果。合约选择的弹性够高，使九十年代的中国免于经济衰退。

余下来还有一个问题：总有一天，农地转作工商业用途的边际价值会下降至均衡点。可能十年之后吧。今天我们见到的县与县之间的激烈竞争会消失吗？答案是这竞争的转弱会出现。然而，有县制度的存在，竞争会转到其他方向去。最可能的新竞争目标是科技的发展。为此我曾建议北京的朋友要紧握增值税，因为科技的引进是最有效的增值法门。

第十节：中国的货币制度与人民币的兴起

朱镕基是个精明的人。虽然职位转来转去，一般的意见，是从一九九三年七月到二〇〇三年三月，他是中国经济的舵手。表面看他是个计划经济者，是个独裁者，也是个不相信市场的人。一九九五年我批评他处理通胀的方法，后来以文章及在电视公开道歉：他对，我错。

我们不能以一个改革者的言论甚至行动来评价他的政绩。他的成败只能以效果衡量。这样量度，朱先生可以拿满分。看似权力欲强，但在他掌政时中央的权力是大幅地下放了。不相信市场，但他在任时国内的市场变得那样彻底地自由，就是崇尚新古典的经济学者也会感动。你可以指责市场有假货，但产品质量的急升大可与当年的日本一较高下，而市场的合约，无论产品的或劳工的，显示着的自由其他地方难得一见。

一九九三年，中国的通货膨胀加剧，人民币暴跌。我在该年五月二十一日发表文章，说控制货币量不会有效，因为无法做到。[注四十二]我指出困难所在，是中国的银行乃出粮机构，有权势的人可以随意"借"钱。于是建议，中国人民银行要负起一间正规中央银行的职责，不提供任何商业借贷。更重要的是：以权力借贷的行为要杜绝。

一九九三年七月一日，朱镕基接管人民银行。掌此职仅两年，但他创立了中国货币制度的架构，并一直监控着这制度的运作，直到二〇〇三年三月从国家总理的职位退休。一九九五年他把人民银行转为正规的中央银行。他控制通胀的方法，是直接地约束借贷与消费，把人民币与美元挂钩。我当时对他的约束办法有怀疑，但也认为可能是斩

[注四十二] 张五常，《权力引起的通货膨胀》，一九九三年五月二十一日，《壹周刊》，转刊于张五常，《二十一世纪看中国的经济革命》，花千树出版，一七五至一七九页。

断权力借贷的唯一办法。受到弗里德曼的影响,我反对人民币挂钩而不浮动。

一九八三年香港的财政司考虑港元采用钞票局的制度,让港元与美元挂钩,我参与了讨论。英国的 Charles Goodhart 建议港元要下一个锚,而弗里德曼支持采用钞票局。人民币怎么办呢?八十年代后期出现不少困难,九十年代初期开始崩溃。我求教过米尔顿好几次,遇上任何关于中国的事,他的时间是非常慷慨的。

米尔顿之见,是像中国那样庞大的国家,不能采用钞票局制度。他认为我提出的把人民币与一篮子物品挂钩原则上可行,但费用会是高的。他的选择,是中国采用美国的无锚货币制,严谨地控制货币量,让汇率自由浮动。

一九九七年,亚洲金融风暴发生后不久,一组来自北京的经济学者邀请我到深圳会谈。他们对中国的前景很忧心。在讨论中我突然间乐观起来,因为意识到朱镕基做对了。只三年他把中国的通胀率从百分之二十以上调整至零,而当时的产品质量正在急升,通缩一定存在。我于是推论,亚洲的金融风暴是人民币突然而又迅速地转强的结果。当时大多数的亚洲国家，包括中国，都钩着美元，所以当中国的通胀骤然间终结，在国际竞争下钩着美元的亚洲小艇纷纷脱钩，因为他们的币值是偏高了。注四十三

一年之后，我更为理解朱镕基的货币制度。他的方法可以理解为给人民币下了一个可以成交的指数为锚。得到朱的启发，我意识到一个国家的货币可以用一篮子物品的物价指数为锚，用不着要有真实物品的储备，条件是央行要有些外汇储备，必要时左右一下，而更重要的是不用货币政策来调控经济。把货币的用途限于货币现象，将汇率与一个可以成交的指数挂钩是不难维持的。

是市场合约的自由与弹性协助中国在九十年代幸免于经济衰退的蹂躏。就是不算当时产品质量的急升，通缩率逾百分之三，而房地产的价格下降了三分之二以上。然而，失业率徘徊于百分之四，

注四十三　当时我没有发表这个解释，因为恐怕扰乱外汇市场。当这解释二〇〇六年四月二十七日发表时，一位曾经专注于该金融风暴的北京朋友惊叫，说我的解释一定对。该风暴出现时，他和同事狂热地找解释，但后来回顾所有解释都不对。见张五常，《铁总理的故事》，二〇〇六年四月二十七日发表于《壹周刊》。

增长率约百分之八。分红合约与件工合约当时盛行，协助了真实工资的自动向下调整。^{注四十四}再者，为了确保他要达到的百分之八的增长率，朱镕基把市场全部放开，大力推行国企的私有化，拿开约束劳动人口流动的限制，也加速了经济决策的向下分散。上马时朱可能是个市场怀疑者，下马之际他必定转为信奉市场了。

回头说中国的货币问题。二〇〇二年在天津南开大学的一次讲话中，我说人民币是世界最强的货币——当时的黑市汇率还低于官价的。^{注四十五}到了二〇〇三年三月，在一篇评论朱退休的文章中，我说人民币那么强劲，两年之内西方的国家会强迫人民币升值——那时黑市与官价汇率大致打平。^{注四十六}这样用黑市与官价汇率的互相运作来估计一种货币的强弱，一九九三与米尔顿研讨过，

注四十四　分红合约有工资自动向下调整的机能。件工合约有同样的弹性，因为有新订单时件工之价往往由劳资双方再洽商。见张五常，《制度的选择》，第四章，第六节，二〇〇二年花千树出版。

注四十五　张五常，《以中国青年为本位的金融制度》，二〇〇二年六月二十日发表于《壹周刊》。

注四十六　张五常，《令人羡慕的困境——朱镕基退休有感》，二〇〇三年三月十一日发表于《苹果日报》。

加上我跟进了地下钱庄的非法交易活动。这些活动的存在，北京当然知道。

外国施压要人民币升值来了，不是两年后，而是四个月后。我坚决地反对人民币大幅升值。理由是如果要改进农民的生活，他们要被鼓励转到工业去。除非农民的生活提升到城市工人的水平，中国的经济改革不能说是成功。多个世纪以来，中国农民的故事永远是血，是苦，是泪与汗。记忆所及，这是第一次农民看到一丝曙光，而人民币汇率的大幅提升会消灭这希望。

一九九一年在斯德哥尔摩，参加科斯获诺贝尔奖的盛会，我对米尔顿说世界将会见到十到二十亿的廉价劳动人口加入国际贸易，二十年后地球的经济结构会有很大的转变。这竞争来临了，而我关心的是虽然中国的工资低廉，比起印度与越南等地还是高出相当多。这些国家也发展得强劲，我当然高兴，理由简单：他们愈富有，跟他们贸易中国赚的钱会愈多。然而，把人民币的国际汇值提升是让赛。很多农民到今天还没有见过真的飞机在天空飞行，人民币升值怎可以改善他们的生活呢？

目前中国有无数的我称为接单厂家的工厂。他们既没有发明专利也没有注册商标，只靠客户交来样板与设计，有单就接。当一个订购者要求复制样板及开价，这要求通常寄到多处，到几个国家也是常有的。我的观点，有大量的事实支持，是农民尝试工业一般由接单工厂做起，学得点技术与知识然后向上爬。感谢蒙代尔，他也曾多次大声疾呼地反对人民币升值。

要清除人民币升值的压力不困难。与其愚蠢地压制人民币的需求——央行目前正在这样做——他们大可取消外汇管制，让人民币大量地流进国际市场。一种货币的下降与上升的压力是不对称的。有下降压力很头痛，但上升压力绝对不坏。让人民币外流国家赚钱，而中国目前的外汇储备泛滥，有需要时可以容易地把人民币买回来。通货膨胀的担心可以用一篮子物品作为人民币之锚而解决了。

得到朱镕基的启发，二〇〇三年我建议，也重复过几次，人民币转用一篮子物品为锚，正确一点地说是以这篮子的可以成交的物价指数为锚。央行不需要有这篮子的物品存货。他们只要担保一个币量可以在指定的市场购得这篮子物品。

这个可以成交的指数容易调整，即是说物价的水平可以容易地调整。物品的选择与比重的分配要慎重考虑，做得对通胀再不会是关心的问题。

把货币钩着一篮子物品，多年前与米尔顿研讨过，而这思维与蒙代尔的货币观是一致的。朱镕基的经验显示，实践的成本不高，因为货币之锚只是个可以成交的物价指数，央行不需要持有这些物品。

北京考虑了我的建议良久，那其实是朱镕基的货币制度加上一点变化。这变化是向旁站开一步，避去与其他国家争吵，对他们说："我们是回复到古老的本位制，只是我们用一个可以成交的物价指数为锚，没有真实物品的储备。这是我们选择的确认自己的币值的方法，与所有其他外币的汇率是自由浮动的。"当然，要防止通胀，以一个可以成交的实物价格的指数为锚，远胜一篮子用纸造的货币。

央行没有接受建议我不感到烦扰，但两三年来他们的操作使我担心。上述提到之外，我的感受是他们要尝试美国的无锚货币制。货币政策早晚会大手采用。这会大幅地增加央行干预经济活动的权力，到后来可能把县制度破坏了。

让我重复上文说过的一个重点。互相竞争的县的权利结构不容易瓦解。任何不明智的政策，侵犯了县的利益而县有权说话的，我不担心。例如我不担心价格管制或租金管制，如果这些管制出现，我敢打赌要不是不被执行，就是执行也不会持久。我担心的是县无权过问的政策。这方面，货币政策居于头痛项目之首。

第十一节：结语

这篇文章我集中于中国做对了什么来解释他们的经济奇迹，想着到结尾时说些负面的话来平衡一下，但写到结尾我不愿意这样做。是中国经济改革的三十周年。中国的传统教我们，一个人生日之际不要把污泥掷到他或她的脸上。也不只是一个人。是一个曾经那么丰富而又有深度的文化。五千年前这文化产出的陶器与玉雕我们今天还没有本领复制出来。为这传统我感到骄傲，而任何人研究过中国的历史与文化，会同意那是人类足以为傲的一个源头。今天，这传统是在复兴了。

这些年北京做出来的大可引以为傲。你可以详尽地批评执掌政权的人，但他们减少了那么多的贫困，工程之庞大与迅速，历史从来没有出现过。我认为这样的成就不会再重复——不管是何地，不管是何时。

我坚信私产与市场对社会的价值，不止四十年了。但我从来没有反对过中国共产党的存在。从第一天起我反对通过民主投票来改革。一九八三年，第一次与一群老同志在北京会面时，我不客气地直言："你们把国家搞得一团糟，要替我把国家修理好。"我们成为好朋友。伤感的是，他们之中多位已经不在了。他们后来做到的，远超我的期望。午夜思回，有时我幻想着要是这些老同志还活着，见到今天的中国，会有怎么样的反应呢？

中国共产党做出来的成果令我拍案！政党历来有困难，困难多多。党员八千万，要怎样安排党的职责与执行党规才对呢？不可思议。

党领导与指挥了改革行动。然而，成功的主要原因还是中国的人民：刻苦，聪明，有耐力。只要能看到明天有希望，他们可以在今天忍受着巨大的艰辛。我不想在这里赞扬中国人，但我没有见过一个民族可以在那么恶劣的环境下那样拼搏——而还在笑。二〇〇四年，在国内的荒山野岭摄影，太太与一个在田中操作的妇人闲谈。这妇人说久不久会有一日有受薪工作，雇主会以大车接送她及其他人到工业园去作园艺。天还未亮起程，天黑后才回家，带着面包与一瓶水，一天的工作可获七美元。我见她在笑，问她为何这般开心。她说生活改进了，有生以来她的植树知识第一次有外间的需求，而女儿刚从大学毕业，找到了一份很好的月薪二百美元的工作。是像这个妇人的人，数以千万计的，把国家建设起来了。

一九七九我发表第一篇中语文章，热衷地下笔是一九八三的秋天开始的。今天在盛年的干部与企业家，那时是大学生。很多读过我写的，所以这些日子，作为一个老人，在国内所到之处，不愁没有免费饭餐吃。跟他们当餐对酒是乐事，也从这些聚会中获得一手的资料来写这篇文章。这里我要以深深的诚意感谢他们，也要再感谢他们的工作，把国家从漫长的黑洞推出来，见到曙光了。

流行的报道说中国的干部例行地贪污，不可能对。他们之中很多有智慧，对国家有贡献。一种竞争的风气使我想到六十年代初期在洛杉矶加州大学作学生时的感受。在一组同学中大家知道或听过谁是谁，对大家的本领互相估计，然后玩那成绩排列的竞争游戏。仿佛没有其他目的，只是要看谁能爬得高一点。

那位到我家来求喝一杯葡萄酒的县长是个例子。他工作拼搏，但工资低——每月约三百美元——使我怀疑是些什么驱使他奔走。是贪污钱吗？是升职吗？是声誉吗？我试图很含蓄地找出他的动力根源。过了好一阵他知道我要问的是什么，说:"教授呀,我只想为国家做点事。"不难想象,气氛环境适当,可以有很多像这位县长的人。

回头说中国奇迹吧。那史无先例的经济制度之外,我选两个现象为奇迹之首。其一是约一九九三开始,长江三角洲出现了爆炸性的经济发展,伸延到国家的中西部去。这个现象出现的时期,开头有人民币的崩溃,有百分之二十以上的通胀,跟着是百分之三强的通缩,而房地产的价格下降了三分之二以上。其二是大约二〇〇〇年起,通缩终结,农民的收入开始爆炸性地上升。从二〇〇〇至二〇〇七,我的估计是农民的人均收入的每年增长率,高达百分之二十。工作年龄的农民,四个有三个转到工商业去了。只要这趋势继续,十年后中国农民的人均收入会与城市的中等人家打平。趋势当然不可靠,但如果真的继续,我的估计是二十年后,中国的经济实力会等于十个日本。

结笔之际,我要对一个我批评过的人致敬。他是朱镕基。老师阿尔钦当年屡次提醒我:成功只能以效果——而不是以热情——来衡量的。上述我排列为首的两项奇迹,都出现于朱先生掌管经济的时期。将来的历史不会忘记这个人。

*　　　*　　　*

不愉快的后记

上文写于二〇〇七年八月。除了中央银行把朱镕基的货币制度左改右动，我当时认为中国经济改革的三十周年有数之不尽的理由要大事庆贺一番。我没有注意到新《劳动合同法》：二〇〇七年六月二十九日通过，二〇〇八年一月一日施行。北京没有征求过县政府的意见。

二〇〇七年十月我收到该新法的文件，只略看内里的九十八条就知道是灾难性。当时正在写一系列关于通胀的文章，要到十二月才有机会评论该新法。十二月十三日发表第一篇，批评该法的文章，支持的声浪高得很。[注四十七] 然而，二〇〇八年一月二十七日，六个政府性质的部门在北京大学举行会议，反对我的说法。我前后写了十一篇评论文章，主要是解释北京不明白的市场与机构或公司之间的关系。这系列文章起不了多少作用：二〇〇八年三月在北京举行的会议中，有关部门显然固执地要推行该法。

[注四十七] 张五常，《新劳动法的困扰》，二〇〇七年十二月十三日发表于《壹周刊》。

基本上，新《劳动合同法》说，雇用劳力或员工的合约再不能自由了。这些合约要服从政府规定的严格条件。超时及假日工资加倍，雇主提供的食宿不能从工资扣除，合约要用文字写出来，员工的假期及福利要这样那样，工会受到鼓励，革职的程序改了——全部是维护劳工的利益，也引进了近于美国大学的终身雇用制：一个员工在一家机构工作了十年就不能被革职，直至退休。

虽然时间刚好吻合，我不敢说中国股市的暴跌是新《劳动合同法》与北京的三月会议引起的。正如牛顿所说，只有上帝才明白股市的变动。注四十八我也不敢说二〇〇八年头两个月的出口急跌，尤其是玩具与成衣，是新《劳动合同法》的效应。雪灾是记忆中最严重的。可以说的是山东的一个地区，约一百二十家韩国人拥有的工厂，在春节假日中悄悄地关闭，员工假后回来见大门锁上，内里无人。该新法对旧机构的损害比新机构为甚，成千上万的在旧工业区的工厂关门，骨牌效应推到工业的后援行业去。员工被革职的无数，不少旧

注四十八　在股市输掉了身家后，牛顿说："我可以算出宇宙物体的运行，但算不出人类发神经。"见 John Carswell, *The South Sea Bubble*（London: Cresset Press, 1960），一三一与一九九页。

工业区的食肆破产。工人有联群上街的行动。

见到工业的发展一时间转暗，北京某部门认为次贷风暴与美国不景是原因。不对，越南、印度、巴基斯坦等地的输出是上升了。没有疑问，新《劳动合同法》触发了工业转移到其他廉价劳力的国家去。好些档次较低的在中国的工业投资者搬家，尤其是搬到越南。有些在外地兴建工厂，可开工时会把客户一并带去。

不能想象北京不知道这些事。他们一定知道。为什么呢？为什么到了二〇〇八年三月，负面效应那么明显，他们还在坚持新《劳动合同法》的执行呢？除了律师与一小撮劳工，所有的人都受损。广东的省长说，政府的政策要考虑到员工、雇主与政府本身的利益，但新《劳动合同法》对这三方面都有损害。明显地，北京的三月会议这位省长之见没有受到欢迎。

我看不到有什么压力团体会因为新《劳动合同法》而获益。几位律师朋友也反对该法，说预期的生意增加补偿不了处理员工问题的麻烦。考虑到该法在中国经济改革三十周年及北京奥运的大日子推出，难以明白。

我有三个可能的解释，最可能是三者的合并，虽然经济逻辑加不起来。其一是北京不知道自二〇〇〇年开始，中国的贫苦农民的收入出现了史无前例的迅速增长。不容易知道。月入人民币一千六百以下的不用报税，流动的劳工一般不报，这些人的收入不易估计。更重要是农村的户籍人口依然多，虽然不少流动去了。如果以农户的总收入除以户籍人口，一个不实的低数字会出现。

二〇〇四年一月，两位中国作者出版了一本赢得国际赞誉的书。这本书提供资料，说中国农民实在苦。注四十九 一年后，世界银行的报告说，中国进入了世界贸易组织后，农民的生活转坏了。这些言论，在中国历史上农民的生活改进得最快的时刻说出，是不负责任的。是的，就是到了二〇〇八年三月三日，林毅夫在上述的北京会议讲话，说中国的收入分配愈来愈不合理。这是他的报告主题。注五十 毅夫是负责农业政策的人，怎可以不知道农民的日子从来没像今天这么好？他怎可以不知道从百分比的增长看，中国的贫富差距这几年正在急速地收窄？

注四十九　陈桂棣与春桃，《中国农民调查》，二〇〇四年一月人民文学出版社。

注五十　《林毅夫称收入分配不合理越来越明显》，二〇〇八年三月七日《新京报》。

新《劳动合同法》的意图是帮助穷人，但二〇〇八年一月十七日我发表文章，推断中国贫民收入的直升线，会因为此法而折下。^{注五十一}这折下是明显地开始出现了。

第二个推出新《劳动合同法》的可能理由，是国家主席胡锦涛提出了要优化结构的观点。^{注五十二}没有人有理由反对，但不幸地，这观点被不少人阐释为要取缔低科技、劳工密集的行业。我们不要忘记经济改革的主旨，是要使贫苦大众脱离饥寒交迫的困境，而在人口那么多的中国，科技的发展是要让低下阶层在下面竞争而把上层的科技推上去的。

最后一个可能的理由，是西方经济学的不良影响。那所谓效率工资理论，其可靠性有疑问，^{注五十三}但回归的经济学博士阐释为工资愈高，工人的产出愈多。如果说有两组生产力完全一样的工人，工

注五十一　张五常，《灾难的先兆——三论新劳动法》，二〇〇八年一月十七日发表于《壹周刊》。

注五十二　胡锦涛提出"科学发展观"。

注五十三　有些人认为效率工资理论源于我的"Why Are Better Seats 'Underpriced'?" *op. cit.*，但我的意思可不是该新理论说的。一个批评效率工资理论的分析可见于张五常，《制度的选择》，二〇〇二年花千树出版，一五六至一五九页。

资较高的一组会产出较多，我可以接受。这只不过是说如果刊物的老板把我的稿酬加倍，我的文章会写得可读一点。但一个雇主究竟要员工在哪个水平操作呢？工资较低的那一组怎样了？为什么最低的工资要让置身事外的政府来决定？

回到这篇文章的主题，我们要问：正在竞争的县的权力怎样了？虽然通过新《劳动合同法》之前没有征求过他们的意见，但我说过，他们对中央上头的不当干预有顽固的弹性抗拒力。他们会怎样应对呢？目前，大部分的县对新《劳动合同法》忙顾左右。可惜这一次不容易抗拒。有三个原因。其一是新法之前有旧劳动法，软性的，基本没有执行。新《劳动合同法》引起人们注意违反旧法的旧账。其二，因为新法中的第十四条（终生雇用条款），雇主与员工要回头看十年的已往。最后，北京建议如果员工起诉雇主，政府提供律师费。一团糟！

如果北京坚持要执行新《劳动合同法》，效果会如何？上文说过的不论，两项发展是肯定的，其实已经开始出现了。其一是企业会采取逃避性的合约安排，不仅是员工合约，企业本身的合约结构也会改变。这会使交易费用上升，对经济发展不利。其二，从事生产的老板会多置机械，解雇那些生产力较弱的员工。目前的情况，是倒闭的大部分是较小的或在"边际"的工厂。这可能使北京认为他们成功地推进科技，减少了劳力密集的产出，但实际上，科技的进步会因为少了下层的劳动力支持而转慢了。

今天，北京的朋友显然忘记了邓小平的对改革过程帮助很大的格言：试一试，看一看。他们应该选几个县来试行新《劳动合同法》，监管与观察他们的表现，与没有推行此法的其他县比较一下，然后才决定去不去马。

中国的情况转变得快，我要指出这后记写于二〇〇八年四月八日。

*　　　　*　　　　*

二〇〇八年五月九日，新《劳动合同法》的实施规则刊于网上，以五月二十为限期，征求公众意见。一些律师认为这些规则是对该法做出修改，希望减少对经济的冲击。五月十二日四川地震，经济问题被搁置了。炎黄子孙的灵气与大自然的摧毁力交上了手。地球上的人看着，深表关怀，也对一个民族意志的凯旋增加了仰慕。

五常，二〇〇八年五月三十一日

芝大研讨会科斯的前言后语

Conference Opening and Closing Remarks by Ronald Coase

从科斯的前言说起

张五常　二〇〇八年八月五日

　　科斯在芝加哥大学举办的"中国经济改革研讨会"圆满地结束了。我不在场，但在场的朋友没有一个不认为是难得一见的成功研讨会议。科斯作后语后，全场站起来鼓掌达三分钟之久，流泪者众，而据说科斯自己也热泪盈眶。是中国经改的三十周年，最成功的研讨会竟然在芝加哥出现，可谓异数。没有谁不同意芝大历来是学术气氛最浓厚的重镇，是此"异数"帮了个大忙吧。不知神州大地要到何年何日才有这样的学术气氛呢？在国内搞学术的朋友要客观地注意一下。炎黄子孙的天赋不下于人，改革三十年，高楼大厦无数，但思想学问还是搞不起！

　　这次参与芝加哥研讨的约半是中国人，出自神州，其中不少算是"土佬"的（一笑），但表现却非常出色。可见土佬既然有天赋，把他们放在适当的气氛环境下，上苍赐予的思想本领就冒出来了。事后科斯有所感慨，说："如果这次会议见到的中国人有代表性，我再不用替中国忧心了！"

老人家把他的诺贝尔奖奖金拿出来搞这次研讨会议，搏到尽。认识了他四十多年，知道他历来的执著与坚持，但毕竟是九十七岁了，我不能不舍命陪君子。为该会议提供的开场文稿我用心地写了一整年，而筹备中的招兵买马，我插手指导，因为老人家的品味我知得清楚：科斯重视真实世界，要知道中国究竟发生了些什么事，对不着边际的理论没有兴趣。为此，我建议多邀请中国的企业家与地区干部，结果是这两组人（约占讲话的四成人马）为该会议增加了无限的光彩。

第一天，老人家清早起床，晚上十一时半才睡觉，电话中显得很兴奋。通常他只能应酬两三个小时，这次我有点恐怕他会累死了，不断地催他休息。跟着的几天他当然不能全日参与，但天天到，静坐聆听，感动着年轻的神州学子。这些学子中不少会执笔叙述他们的所见所感，我不多说了。

科斯作了前言，也作了后语。前者是事前用心写好的；后者只写了片刻，讲时不依文稿，情之所至，随意地说了些心中话——这是不少人哭了出来的原因。这后语要等他们整理好录音才能刊登。我征求得老人家同意，在这里先刊出他的引言文稿——七月十四日的开场话。前思后想，决定刊登全文，在《信报》发表用不着翻译了。如下：

I now have the very pleasant task of welcoming you to this Conference on China's Economic Transformation. When Steven Cheung wrote in 1982 his pamphlet for the Institute of Economic Affairs in London on the question "Will China go capitalist?" a question that he answered in the affirmative, I was one of the few people who agreed with him. But I thought in terms of 100 or 200 years, not 25 or 30 years. What happened in China was a complete surprise to me, its scale, its character and speed – which means that I did not understand what was going on. I therefore determined to hold a conference that would uncover the facts about this extraordinary series of events. We sought out those best able to inform us, academics, businessmen, government officials, about the facts about what happened. I think we succeeded. We have a series of fine papers that greatly enlighten us about what has happened in the years since 1978. As we intent to publish an edited version of these papers (and of the discussions) in a book, they will inform a much wider audience. Of course, although we will learn a great deal about what happened, it is not to be expected, although some things will be made clear, that there will be complete agreement in the views expressed – nor is it desirable that there should be. A subject in which everyone says the same thing is a dead subject and one which will not progress. Competition in the market for ideas is as valuable as in the market for goods. The truth is found as a result of the clash of ideas. And it will be so at this conference.

Our first paper by Steven Cheung will be delivered by him on DVD. It is long (about 2 hours) and I decided to divide it into two parts, each about an hour in length with an interval with refreshments in between. Unfortunately, one of our important discussants, Professor Mundell, will not be able to attend on the first day but will give his views on Tuesday morning. I should explain here that while I speak as though I organized this conference, in fact all I did was to have the idea that such a conference would be a good thing. The actual organization of the conference was carried out by Ning Wang, assisted more recently by Lennon Choy and Marjorie Holme. I have been largely a spectator and admirer of their work. I should also say that, approaching 98 years of age later this year, I get extremely tired and almost certainly will not be able to attend all the sessions. But those who present papers at sessions I do not attend should realize that my absence is in no sense of judgment on the worth of their papers.

I now turn to Steven Cheung's talk. I came to know Steven when he came to Chicago from UCLA in 1967 on a fellowship and was later in 1968 appointed an assistant professor. I don't remember how we met. But when we did, we formed an immediate bond and we had the most enjoyable and productive talks together. Unfortunately for Chicago, he decided to leave Chicago and go to the University of Washington where he had as colleagues Douglass North and Yoram Barzel. However, our relationship did not end and Steve wrote a series of splendid articles published in the Journal of Law and Economics of which I was editor. Then, in 1981, Steve received an offer from the University of Hong Kong. I urged him to accept. I thought it would be a fine place to observe what was happening in China. Just how valuable it would be I did not then realize. But you will learn from his talk what he has gained from his close observation of events in China over the years. I won't hold up this really important talk any longer. So here we have Steven Cheung speaking on China's Economic Transformation.

整篇前言的重点，当然是第一段的最后几句。太重要了，我要另文申述。这里刊出全文，是要指出其他两点，远为次要的，但中国的学子们要跪下来学习一下。

第一点是九十七岁的科斯，其思想的清晰，推理逻辑的紧密，今天在网上大吵大闹的青年拍马也跟不上。为什么呢？说二三十岁的脑子机能比不上九十七岁的，上帝不会同意吧。那是为什么？我认为那是起于科斯从小就接受了英国传统的学问修养，看事客观，下笔时心平气和。毫无磨斧痕迹的文字，要写到这样才算是真的到家。

第二点是科斯的英文实在好。四十年前以文笔知名天下的哈里·约翰逊，清楚地对我说，论英语的文字功力，没有谁比得上科斯。懂英文的中国人可能认为科斯的文字火花不足，或变化不够，或潇洒欠奉，但我是过来人，下过苦功，知道这样的文字看似平凡，其实高不可攀。直写、清晰，既不转弯，也不卖弄，有英国人的幽默（例如第三句），而更重要是诚恳与善意溢于纸上。

年多前读到香港搞语文教育的专家的文字，不管是中还是英，老实说，读来不舒服，其他不便多说。看来香港的语文教育要从零开始了。

长眠的阐释——
科斯的后语会进入历史吗?

张五常　二〇〇八年九月十六日

　　科斯在芝加哥大学举办的"中国经济改革研讨会议"今年七月十八日终结时,作了简短的后语。事前他花了十分钟写了一点初稿,但讲时没用上,只是毫无准备地说了一些话。这些话感人,听者流泪,站起来鼓掌两三分钟,而科斯自己也热泪盈眶。王石当时在场,事后给我一个短信,说:"切身感受科斯老教授对中国的真诚关怀。"

　　这个没有文稿的后语按录音翻出来了,科斯说要修改一番才发表。但这一次——只这一次——我不尊重他老人家,一意孤行地在这里刊登原文。理由有二。其一是他修改后的将不是现场有感而发的话。其二是因为有感而发,这后语有机会打进将来中国的经济历史去。这里先发表,过后我会放进自己的结集中,档案明确,有凭有据,将来写中国历史的要怎样取舍是他们的选择。

　　下面先刊英语原文,前思后想,认为要补加翻译。难译,是由我翻的,其中"长眠"(long

sleep）一词如何阐释有争议。不便问科斯，但按上文下理读者或可解通。全文如下（是录音翻出的没有文稿的讲话，文字上这里那里有点沙石）：

Although I knew that I would have to say something at the end of the conference, I am nonetheless taken by surprise when I had to do it and I am not sure I know what I am going to say. Which puts me in the same position you are in, you don't know what I am going to say.

This conference has clearly been a great success. I wanted this conference to take place because what happened in China was a great surprise to me. If you are surprised at what happens, it means you don't understand it, and I don't understand it. And I thought we should have a conference in which the participants in the events in China could speak as against having people who didn't take part in the events and whose opinions weren't always very reliable. So we tried to get businessmen, government officials, academics who had been involved in the transformation to speak to us.

I must say I had belief in China's future for a long

time. As a young boy I read Marco Polo, and just as he was amazed at what he found, so was I, and I felt here is a country with great potential but somehow didn't achieve it. And it was a puzzle to me as to why didn't achieve it and I was very surprised when, in the period after 1978 it seemed it was going to achieve its potential. And what I heard in this conference has confirmed this view. I now have a feeling that the events which were set in motion in 1978 will be a great success.

However, human beings have a great capacity for messing things up. You will understand that, when I describe what happened in my life. When I was born in 1910, the industrial revolution has been absorbed in Europe. The social system seemed stable. And what happened when I was four the Great War opened. It was a stupid war. It achieved nothing worthwhile, in fact it did harm, and millions of men were killed. People lost faith in the social system and then communism came in. It was absolute disaster and it destroyed changes in attitude in people and resulted in a world a good deal worse than it was when I was born.

Now if you think of the present situation, that is, we have a situation in which everything seems be going along well, that's what I'd learnt from this conference. When I wrote the foreword to Steven Cheung's book of English articles, I said that the struggle for China is the struggle for the world, that I truly believe. Well, will we actually achieve this desirable result? Well of course I will never know although you will. All I can do is to say that our discussions carried out will make it possible. But to make it possible as we know is not enough. The political regime has to carry out its actions. Whether it will or not, I don't know. All I can do is to hope it will and to wish you well in the next hundred years. And I can now thank you...thank you.

What you are going to do, as I am sure you are, is to bring about desirable results. And I would think of you now, because it would be difficult to do much thinking in that long sleep which I am going to have. But it makes me happy to think that you will, as is shown by what you said in this conference, make the efforts. That makes me happy and I thank you."

中译如下：

"虽然我知道在这会议终结时我要说一些话，事到临头我却惊讶于自己一定要说，而又不能肯定要说些什么。这就把我放在你们的位置上：你们不知道我将会说些什么。

"这个研讨会议取得巨大的成功是清楚的。我要这个会议出现，因为中国发生了的事给我很大的惊奇。如果你对发生的事感到惊奇，是说你不明白。我不明白。于是想，我们应该有一个研讨会议，让参与过中国发展的人说话，这会比那些没有参与过的人的见解来得可靠。我们于是尝试找那些参与过中国经济改革的商人、干部与学者来对我们说。

"必须说的是我相信中国的前途有很久的时日了。做孩子时我读马可·波罗，正如他吃惊于所遇，我也是，而我当时觉得那是个潜力庞大的国家，不知为什么没有发挥出来。对我来说，不能发挥这潜力是一个谜，而使我震惊的，是一九七八之后的迹象显示，这潜力仿佛开始体现了。这个会议我听到的，证实着这个观点。现在我有这样的感受：一九七八启动了的发展，将会是个伟大成就。

"然而，人类有很大的可以把事情搞得一团糟的能耐。告诉你我一生遇到的，你会明白。一九一〇我诞生的时候，欧洲正在神往于工业革命。社会的制度看来是稳定的。但四岁时，世界大战爆发了。是一个愚蠢的战争。争取到的毫无价值，事实上造成损害，百万计的人死了。人们对社会的制度失却了信心，共产制度于是来临。绝对是大灾难，这制度毁灭了人们的态度转变，效果是世界变得比我出生时坏很多。

"现在你们想想目前的情况，那就是我们面对的情况，看来进展得好，而这是我在这次会议中学得的。当我为张五常的英语论文结集写前言时，我说中国的奋斗是世界的奋斗。这一点我是深信的。但我们真的会争取到良好合意的效果吗？这问题的答案我永远不知道，但你们是会知道的。我能做的只是说，我们的研讨增加了这合意效果的可能。然而，我们知道增加这可能不足够。政治系统要以行动带来实践。是成是败我不知道。我只能希望这系统会履行，也希望今后百年你们万事如意。现在我可以感谢你们……感谢你们。

"你们将会做的，我肯定你们会做的，是要带来良好的合意效果。现在我会想着你们，因为在我将要有的长眠中多想什么不容易。但当我想到你们将会尽力而为——会议中你们这样表达过——我高兴。你们使我高兴,我感谢你们。"

朋友,人非草木,你哭了吗?有点争议的,是科斯在最后说自己将要长眠,有两个解法。其一是会议开了五天,他累了,要好好地睡一长觉。其二是他近九十八岁了,快要离开人世,永远地长眠去也。哪个解法才对呢?我知道答案,不说,读者自己阐释吧。

科斯的思想对中国改革的贡献我说过多次了。他对中国的真诚关怀我知道了四十年——他当年千叮万嘱要我回到香港去给中国的同胞解释经济制度的运作。今天所见,神州未富先骄,为争取自己利益而不顾大局的人那么多,效与愿违的政策层出不穷,科斯的希望能得到实践的机会不大。但如果他的希望真能体现,我认为上述的感人后语会在将来的中国历史上占有一个可爱的注脚。